At least we're talking. As Nathan Kerr notes in his chapter, one of the characteristics of modernism is to define the boundary and label everything outside as the enemy. If the Wesleyan-Holiness folk are to have a voice in the future of the church, we cannot afford to treat everything that is postmodern and emergent as an enemy. God has never been a "boundaried" God. Our friends in this book have launched a needed conversation. Friends, let's talk.

—Dan Boone
President, Trevecca Nazarene University

This volume provides more open dialogue about the positive contributions and the concerns of postmodernism from a Wesleyan perspective than virtually any book currently on the market! Individuals and churches will find in its pages provocative and helpful tools with which to understand and interact with the changes taking place in our world today.

—Charles W. Christian
Pastor, North Seattle Church of the Nazarene

The writers in this volume are postmoderns or those who are uniquely positioned to understand postmodernism. This volume gives us an opportunity to hear their voices and dialogue with their ideas so that we can better discern what the church might look like in our changing culture. I encourage you to read this volume with a spirit of curiosity and expectation.

—Vicki Copp
Professor, Nazarene Theological Seminary

Easy to read and irenic in its approach, this book is a useful introduction both to those who want to find out what postmodernism is and those who want to see how a postmodern discussion can be fruitfully conducted in the church.

—Timothy J. Crutcher
Professor, Southern Nazarene University

Postmodern and Wesleyan? is a nuanced and robust approach to the tectonic shift in culture and the church in which we currently find ourselves. I thoroughly enjoyed the dialogical approach that encourages and stimulates even more conversation on the journey we find ourselves in today.

—Dave L. Curtiss
USA/Canada Youth Ministry Coordinator, Church of the Nazarene

Many say we are entering a new age, the age of "postmodernism." One of the frightening things with a change of such magnitude is that v⁓   actually know what the outcome will be. This book does not p⁓   ⁓ers. If anything, it asks more questions! It helps you th⁓   lural. Hence it is written for discussion in ch⁓   cell groups, and pretty much any group⁓   ing church in the 21st century.

..s Deventer
. ɩvaznet Moderator

Reading this book reflects the kinds of conversations many from the Wesleyan tradition have been having over the last few years about postmodernity, the emergent church, and the role these things play in the lives and communities of our particular Christian tradition. The multicontributor format of this book gives you a true flavor of this dynamic conversation and invites you to do more than just read it, but to dialogue with it and participate in this growing conversation.

—James Diggs
Pastor of the Corridor, a Nazarene community between Baltimore and DC
Founding Contributor of EmergentNazarenes.com

The scribes and pastor-scholars contributing to this book helpfully move us beyond just how we think about God, Jesus, the church, and the world and call us to imagine how our ideas of God, Jesus, the Holy Spirit, and the Body of Christ become flesh in these times.

—Jamie Gates, M.Div. Ph.D.
Director, Center for Justice and Reconciliation
Professor, Point Loma Nazarene University

This collection of essays and discussion starters is just what is needed for the church to engage in a serious conversation over the role of the gospel in a postmodern world. What is postmodernism? What is the church in a postmodern world? What is the mission of the church in this world, and what about other religions? All of these issues and more become occasions for discussion among the people of God. This is a wonderful tool for discussion groups and Sunday School classes who are trying to make sense out of a concept and what seems to be a way of being in the world.

—Stephen G. Green
W. N. King Chair of Theology
Professor, Southern Nazarene University

Postmodern and Wesleyan? seeks to create a hospitable space for thoughtful dialogue on current shifts in culture and thought. The writers practice a Wesleyan way of approaching the truth that is more conversational than combative, more generous than suspicious, and more loving than fearful. At its best, this study book models that Wesleyan way for the rest of us, calling us all to enter into this critical conversation together.

—Mark Hayse
Professor, MidAmerica Nazarene University

I love this new book! As a pastor, I really appreciate this honest attempt to relate to postmodern/emergent issues from a Wesleyan point of view. The thought-provoking questions at the end of each chapter were a special joy. They drew me into the conversation. In the end, the format made my approach less linear and modern and more random and conversational.

—Robert Luhn
Pastor, Othello Church of the Nazarene

The potential for telling the Good News in the language of our postmodern culture will be enhanced if the "translation tips" gathered in this collection of essays are heeded. Like any helpful translation guide, don't leave home without it.

—Alan Lyke
Chaplain and Professor, Nazarene Bible College

Stepping fully into the fray of postmodernism, *Postmodern and Wesleyan?* offers a richly diverse primer on postmodernism by using one of our "forgotten" Wesleyan means of grace—*conversation*. Postmodernism will continue to elude us as long as we keep the "conversation" away from the gospel and the Church bearing witness to the Good News. The conversation of this primer on postmodernism moves us in the right direction.

—K. Steve McCormick
William M. Greathouse Chair for Wesleyan-Holiness Theology
Nazarene Theological Seminary

This collection of essays is a helpful entry into a deeper understanding of postmodernism from a Wesleyan perspective. As a whole it is an invitation into a lively conversation that will serve Wesleyans well as we try to help a church that is primarily modern offer the good news of Christ to a world that is primarily postmodern.

—Mary R. Paul
Vice President for Spiritual Development, Point Loma Nazarene University

Postmodern and Wesleyan? is an excellent look into how Wesleyan life, practice, and theology can speak powerfully in the postmodern world. This book will aid anyone who wants to explore or better understand the potent synergies between Postmodernism and Wesleyanism.

—Kevin Rector
Pastor, Wausau Church of the Nazarene

Postmodern and Wesleyan? is a dialogue, not a debate. So if you're looking for arguments to win debates, this isn't the book for you. But if you're seeking understanding of the mission and practice of the Christian church in the Wesleyan-Holiness tradition, regardless of which side of postmodernity you reside, then *Postmodern and Wesleyan?* not only will be a good read but also an excellent conversation partner.

—Ed Robinson
President, MidAmerica Nazarene University

Postmodern and Wesleyan? is an invitation to an important conversation in the church among people who are confronted with the problems and possibilities of postmodernism. Within its pages is a willingness to listen to the heartbeat of people who are caught in a culture that alternatively confuses and inspires. Those who read this book will be better able to engage culture, not in fear and anger, but with hope and creativity.

—Henry W. Spaulding II
Professor, Nazarene Theological Seminary

Postmodern and Wesleyan? is an excellent resource for your small group or Sunday School class. The essays provide stimulating insights from the past and investigate possibilities for our tomorrows. The probing questions at the end of each chapter will penetrate your assumptions and engage your class in life-shaping discussions.

—Woodie Stevens
SDMI Director, Church of the Nazarene

The essays in *Postmodern and Wesleyan?* go far beyond a mere description of postmodernism. They focus on a multitude of topics, including the authority of Scripture, soteriology, religious pluralism, politics, and science. The authors do not argue for hard and fast conclusions. Instead, they leave the door open for many perspectives. I highly recommend this volume, and I envision it will have many uses in our local congregations.

—W. Thomas Umbel
Professor, Nazarene Bible College

pOSTMODERN aND wESLEYAN?

eXPLORING tHE bOUNDARIES aND pOSSIBILITIES

rESPONSES bY lEONARD sWEET

jAY rICHARD aKKERMAN
tHOMAS jAY oORD
bRENT d. pETERSON
eDITORS

BEACON HILL PRESS
OF KANSAS CITY

Copyright 2009
By Beacon Hill Press of Kansas City

ISBN 978-0-8341-2458-5

Printed in the
United States of America

Cover Design: J.R. Caines
Internal Design: Sharon Page

10 9 8 7 6 5 4 3 2 1

Dedicated to
Lauren, Hailey, and Parker Akkerman
Sydnee, Lexi, and Andee Oord
Noah and Alexis Peterson
our undergraduate and graduate students,
both on campus and online,
and all citizens of God's kingdom and
to our companions in our postmodern world.

cONTENTS

fOREWORD I

Jay Akkerman, Thomas Jay Oord, and Brent Peterson explore the many facets of postmodernism. They do this in relation to the Church, the gospel, and the missional expression of the Church's life and ministry. Using the interplay of conversation as a means to engage a wide variety of topics, this trio guides the Church into a fertile field of exploration, discussion, and innovative response.

This work is accented by the voices of scholars, students, and ministers. The result is thoroughness in both scope and sequence. The authors of each section bring their experiences, values, and commitments into play as they draw from their Wesleyan background to communicate their perspectives.

Basing their conversational approach on John Wesley's preference for dialogue and conversation, the contributors explore different postmodern motifs in ways that are not only responsible but also encourage readers to voice their own reactions and responses.

All conversations are predicated on the possibility of community. Indeed, without community, conversation is not likely to exist. Instead, participants end up shouting at each other across the bridgeless expanse of misunderstanding, ignorance, or resistant disagreement. Thus, it is important at the very outset for readers to recognize this device. Indeed, the contents of this creative text must be seen for what they are: *an exchange of thoughts, opinions, and feelings*. With this in mind, then, a conversation is not a didactic teaching of the Church with an apostolic imprimatur. Instead, it is an enriching exposure to observations, deductions, and insights based on careful analysis and scrutiny.

Clearly, in a text that engages, from a Wesleyan perspective, a multifaceted subject such as a postmodern approach to the gospel, the Church, and the experience of street-level Christendom, there are bound to be large differences of opinion. Fortunately, engaging conversations imply certain characteristics, one of which is thoughtful expertise. On this front, the contributors to this work bring a vast array of both interest and experience.

If this is your first foray into this complex subject matter, you may encounter ideas that at first glance seem quite different from traditional or conventional expressions and definitions. One of the contributors to this text, Jon Middendorf, offers the following as beneficial bridgework between the established, often unexamined, assumptions that frequently calcify into conventional wisdom:

- Shouldn't the Church—the people of God—share God's willingness to move, adjust, and have genuine conversation? Shouldn't we resist the temptation to crystallize our statements of belief in ways that inhibit, stifle, or outlaw exploration and discovery?

- Words aren't perfect. They cannot contain all that we might want to say about our infinite God. But words in conversation and dialogue are more likely to produce fruit.

It is my prayer that this book hopefully will provoke creative thinking that will motivate our pastors to attempt new methodologies as they stay true to the holiness message.

—Nina Gunter
General Superintendent, Church of the Nazarene

fOREWORD II

Following a Sunday morning service in which we had experienced a profound sense of God's Word speaking to the community of faith, a good and faithful man spoke to me. A well-educated man, a professional, heart-deep in the church, a husband and father of young children, his voice carried a sense of urgency.

"Pastor," he said, "please do not speak anymore about the subject of postmodernism. The more you talk about that, the more people will believe it, and it could undermine the faith of our young people."

A passing reference to "shifts in the ways people hear the Word of God" seemed to be the only item in the sermon he could recall. For him, it implied a "belief system," an "alternative view of God," a disturbing shift being imposed on the theology of the church.

Over the next several months, and after repeated lunchtime conversations, he began to talk about his own experiences in postmodernism. This son of the church, a third-generation believer, a passionate Christian, began to grapple with his own shifting worldview.

Discussing postmodernism is not an easy conversation for some. It suggests a sinister threat to the conservative theological and biblical interpretations that have characterized Wesleyan-Arminianism. But postmodernism is not so much a theological issue as it is a shift in philosophical presuppositions that determine "how we know."

Postmodernism has less to do with today, than it has to do with how we know it is today. And it is not finished. In spite of much consensus on the variety of definitions of postmodernism, by its very nature as descriptive of the changes that are occurring in the ways we know, it is not yet a "fixed" perspective.

I love the discussions in this book. They are enlightening, challenging, sometimes even disturbing. But they cannot be fixed! The final definitions and explanations of postmodernism and its impact on theology, the church, the world, education, and any one of a number of other disciplines and discussions will not be completed until after all of the writers and the current readers of this text are dead.

Postmodernism is not a fixed "ism." It is not a "belief." It is not a position one holds. It is a description of the shifting ways we know, perceive, and communicate. It is influencing the beliefs of the church

13

because the ways we come to faith are undergoing changes, as determined by the rapidly changing worldviews of the people who make up this global community of humankind.

We in the Church do not need to fear postmodernism, but we do need to know that the world is changing. And that must, and inevitably will, change the way we do our work. Whether we are postmodern or not, or whether we want to be or not, we live in a world different from the world of two decades ago. And yet, (God the Father is still on the throne, Christ is still the Head of the Church, and the Spirit is still the sanctifying Presence in the Church and in his people.)

Things are changing, and they are changing rapidly. In times like this, we want to know what is still true. That is the reason we need this conversation. I applaud the contributors to this book for their willingness to help us think through some of the things that will keep us steady when the sands of time are shifting under our feet.

—Jesse C. Middendorf
General Superintendent, Church of the Nazarene

iNTRODUCTION

Change is in the air. Many people sense something uncommonly different. The change they see and feel and imagine is more than simply whatever is supposedly new and improved. This change entails a radically different way of looking at life. The most common word to describe this change is "postmodernism."

To some, postmodernism is a dream becoming reality. To others, it's a nightmare they hope will soon end. No matter what a person's view, it is difficult to deny that many Christians—including many in the Church of the Nazarene—are interested in what it means to be postmodern.

Contemporary prophets promote many forms of postmodernism. We hear of postmodern worship, postmodern liturgy, postmodern preaching, postmodern evangelism, and postmodern theology. Sometimes the label "postmodern" gets slapped on the latest thing. Other times, the label represents a fundamentally novel way of living and thinking. It can be difficult to distinguish the latest thing from a genuine paradigm shift.

For many, postmodernism is more than a fad or a juvenile rebellion against tradition. Many sense that something is changing, but they have difficulty articulating just what that something is.

The themes or characteristics one person describes as postmodern are often not what another person means by postmodern. Diversity reigns. A chorus of voices—some in favor, some not—fill the sanctuary.

But diversity can be a blessing rather than a curse. Diversity can be the impetus for creative transformation. We need criteria, of course, for deciding when diversity is helpful and when it hinders. But we need not label everything in the past as "modern" and therefore bad. And everything new or "postmodern" is not good. How can churches move ahead when their members include both those steeped in modernity and those exploring the boundaries and possibilities of postmodernity?

Postmodern and Wesleyan? Exploring the Boundaries and Possibilities is both an exploration and an internal dialogue. Essays explore various dimensions of postmodernism as they relate to the theology, church practices, communities, mission, and structures of the

Church of the Nazarene. Each essay writer is a member of the denomination.

Postmodern and Wesleyan? is divided into four main sections, with six to eight chapters in each. After each section, a critical response is offered by a respected leader who believes at least some caution is needed for at least some postmodern ideas. And Leonard Sweet, a respected Wesleyan leader and writer on issues of postmodernism, concludes each section with comments meant to continue the conversation. The entire book is offered to induce readers to continue and deepen the conversation about what postmodernism might mean for contemporary Christians.

This book meets the growing interest and need of Wesleyans in general and, more specifically, leaders in the Church of the Nazarene. This need involves engaging constructively the ideas and proposals of postmodernism. The book fills a huge hole and offers a voice to some of the most creative thinkers in the movement. Because of space constraints, the editors regret that many other voices exploring what it means to be postmodern could not be included.

While exploring postmodernism, our book does not pretend to offer *the* proper Wesleyan response to what it should mean to be postmodern. It is not authoritative or definitive in this sense. And it does not speak for the denomination. But *Postmodern and Wesleyan?* does represent serious forays into ways of thinking and acting that are of immense contemporary interest.

The essays in this book are not caustic, divisive, or derogatory. While authors will be critical of dimensions of what they consider modern or premodern, they ultimately attempt to offer hope, point toward positive alternatives, or be constructive.

This book is not meant to destroy and leave the reader stranded in the flatlands. In many ways, the book invites churches, pastors and laity—young and old—to explore how the faith might best be shaped in the present and for the future.

Postmodern and Wesleyan? Exploring the Boundaries and Possibilities is an opportunity for Christians to wrestle with the questions many have wanted to ask but were afraid to raise. It provides a forum for engaging issues that are both important and difficult. It serves as an important conversation piece in helping Christians decide the direction they must go to witness to the good news Jesus Christ declares about the love of God.

pART I

tHE pOSTMODERN cONVERSATION/ sHIFTING cULTURE

1 wHY tALK aBOUT pOSTMODERNISM?

jON mIDDENDORF

As members of the Wesleyan tradition, we have conversation and dialogue written into our DNA. We are an unfolding story whose chapters are marked by important dialogues and debates.

Every major move within our maturing faith community has been fueled by a multitude of voices. Often these voices have co-operated and rejected one-sided dictation or monologues. At their best, these conversations have been bathed in prayer and attentive to God's leadership.

There are dangers that come from listening to a multitude of voices. But those dangers highlight our need to rely upon the God who participates and collaborates along with us. We believe that God gently leads and guides along the way.

The books included in our Bible were not selected by an edict issued from one booming voice. Instead, our Bibles emerged through meetings and councils. Consensus was reached after conversations, dialogue, arguments, and even shouting matches.

The Protestant Reformation demonstrated the hunger for partnership and shared responsibility. Passionate believers insisted on the right of the congregation to be involved in the dialogue about faith, the Church, the world, and the nature of God.

John Wesley understood the power of dialogue. Wesley's emphasis on band, society, and class meetings demonstrated his conviction that character was formed in relationship, not in a silent, conversationless vacuum. He believed that conversation in community really mattered.

Phineas F. Bresee cobbled together varied and disparate faith communities in the hopes of fashioning a critical mass. He and other early leaders hoped to establish a new denomination, wide and broad enough to encompass people of diverse opinions. Many early leaders in the Church of the Nazarene placed a higher premium on community than theological uniformity.

The importance of community is evident in how we in the denomination think about the Bible. We talk about God's working to inspire various writers and God's inspiration for our interpretation. Conversation is present even, or perhaps especially, in how we understand the role of Scripture.

A healthy discussion of any important topic—faith, culture, Church, the nature of God, and so on—requires our involvement. This is more than an opportunity; it's part of our identity. We are "theology by public discourse, theology as public discourse" people.

As those who rely upon conversation and dialogue, we are vulnerable to the same problems that threaten all viable conversations. For instance, (we must resist the tendency to allow the loudest and angriest voices to have more influence. We must resist uncharitable interpretations of what others say. But we must not allow these problems to distract us from our calling to continue to discuss our theology.)

God is a conversation partner whom we ought to imitate. While God's character and basic dreams for creation never change, God is also dynamic and interactive. God is always ready and willing to move at a moment's notice to reach out to creation. God makes it possible for us to respond.

Shouldn't the Church—the people of God—share God's willingness to move, adjust, and have genuine conversation? Shouldn't we resist the temptation to crystallize our statements of belief in ways that inhibit, stifle, or outlaw exploration and discovery?

Words aren't perfect. They cannot contain all that we might want to say about our infinite God. But words in conversation and dialogue are more likely to produce fruit.

Monologue and dictation can be weapons of violence when in the wrong hands. We live among a generation with an aversion to truth dictated by one, autocratic voice. And one-way discourse heightens the possibility that we will be misunderstood by those whom we most want to help.

Clearly God does not need our protection. God reaches out sometimes despite our words. (But honest conversation can generate new discoveries and new possibilities as we listen faithfully to each other and to God's still, small voice.)

Religious dictators have fewer blind followers in our postmodern era. Postmodern people have grown up watching the failures of local, national, and international religious leaders. Many today have more faith in gathered wisdom. This wisdom emerges from the synergy between those in conversation.

Postmodern Christians have grown increasingly frustrated by the Church's lack of familiarity with and lack of desire to dialogue with the broader culture. In the spirit of our Wesleyan heritage, these postmodern believers hope that those outside of church walls will be treated as something other than a threat or an enemy.

(Many postmodern Christians have a deep desire to reenter neighborhoods, towns, and cities as the people of God. This reentering is not done with a posture that would have us pointing fingers, however. It is a reentering in conversation, with a genuine interest in people and places all too often considered beyond our church walls and responsibility.)

(Perhaps postmodern Christians can return to an understanding of the phrase "Holiness Tradition" that will release and reenergize them. For too long "holiness" has been a kind of wall keeping us separated from a culture we have deemed inherently evil. But this understanding of holiness not only puts us in danger of losing touch with postmodern believers but also denies our part of what is distinctive about our Wesleyan heritage.

We are called to risk deep and meaningful relationships with the broader culture. We are called to be people of conversation: people who dare to believe that the truth—not limited to what might be "inside" me or you—can be discovered in a dialogue that allows space and grace for the other. In that kind of dialogue we find that God has been present even before we arrived. And God guides and breathes new life into situations we feared beyond our reach.

Perhaps postmodernism helps us remember that we must enter anew in conversation with others. And this conversation involves both listening and speaking in faith, hope, and love.

Your story: Describe some of the major shifts in your life as a Christian. What impact did these shifts have and how did you handle them?

qUESTIONS

1. Why are some people nervous about any conversations about things theological and spiritual? Like politics, why is religion sometimes a taboo subject among friends and family?

2. Why do Christians have a hard time disagreeing? What does this say about us?

3. A classic tenet within Wesleyan churches has been "on essentials we will agree, on nonessentials we may disagree, but we must always love." Why is this so hard? What is at stake?

4. Why are some persons nervous about the conversation with the broader culture?

aPPLICATION

In light of this chapter and its topics, how might you act differently? Think differently? Feel differently? Relate differently?

a bIG tENT
tHE gENEROUS
oRTHODOXY oF
wESLEYANISM

t. sCOTT dANIELS

We can learn something important for today by looking at what the Bible says about a church in the city of Ephesus. Guarding against what some call the "Ephesus Syndrome" is one of the strengths of faith communities rooted in the Wesleyan tradition.

Of the seven cities addressed in chapters 2 and 3 of the Book of Revelation, it is likely the church in Ephesus faced the greatest pressures of change and political turmoil. John the Revelator praises the Ephesian church for standing up against a pagan culture, false prophets, leadership instability, and the powerful lure of the empire.

Yet, in the midst of being praised for their persistence in keeping the faith, the Ephesian Christians are rebuked for abandoning "the love [they] had at first" (2:4, NRSV). In their zeal for theological and moral purity, they lost the centrality of Christian love.

The reader of this letter is left with a question: is there a connection between the church's zeal for guarding its boundaries and its lost spirit of love? Can a community so focus on maintaining the orthodoxy of its theology that it loses the ability to reflect the character of God?

Although John Wesley did not coin the following, it is often associated with the spirit of his thought: "In essentials, unity. In nonessentials, liberty. In all things, charity." This quote sums up what Wesley called a catholic or universal spirit. Although he acknowledged great differences in the theological traditions of his day, Wesley held fast to the idea that love is the defining characteristic of the Christian spirit.

I like to refer to Wesleyans as people with a "big tent." This does not mean that Wesleyan churches are like circuses. (Although there have been times when that descriptor would apply!) Rather, to have a big tent is to allow space for diverse "nonessential" opinions.

Let me give two examples of how the big tent has been lived out in Wesleyan traditions. Then I'd like to show how this aspect of the Wesleyan spirit fits with some postmodern sensibilities.

The first example of the big-tent spirit of Wesleyanism is the manner in which many Wesleyan denominations formed. Historically, many Wesleyan and Holiness denominations did not arise as splits from a mother tradition. They formed instead by the merging of smaller groups with a common theological vision and passion.

Wesley himself did not intend to break from his Anglican denominational roots. But the formation of the Methodist tradition arose in large part after the Church of England refused to ordain ministers in the United States that Wesley had mentored.

The Church of the Nazarene does not think of itself as a split from Methodism. Instead, it formed through several mergers, including the one at Pilot Point, Texas, in 1908. Disparate groups from the Western, Eastern, and Southern States shared a commission "to preserve and propagate Christian holiness as set forth in the Scriptures, through the conversion of sinners, the reclamation of backsliders, and the entire sanctification of believers."[1]

In the merger negotiations of those groups, a big tent of charity was required to overcome theological differences. Early Holiness Christians often disagreed over theological and social issues. In these arguments, concessions were frequently made on cultural differences and nonessential theological matters. Concession for the sake of unity has been more the rule than the exception in the development of denominations in the Wesleyan tradition.

A second example of the big-tent spirit is the unifying way many doctrines in Wesleyan denominations are articulated. Although there are many areas of diverse theological opinion from which to choose, let me highlight three that have recently tended to be highly divisive.

(The first area of diverse theological opinion has to do with the nature of the Bible. Almost universally, Wesleyan denominations affirm that the Scriptures are divinely inspired. Wesleyans also recognize, however, the divine-human synergy involved in the process of the Bible's formation and authorship. Because of this, most Wesleyan statements of faith shy away from articulating a strict inerrancy view of the Bible. Viewing the Bible as infallible on matters of salvation rather than inerrant on all matters allows a "big tent" for discussion and reflection to occur on the various types of literature contained in the Bible.)

A second area of diverse theological opinion has to do with science and creation. Wesleyan traditions consistently affirm God's role as Creator of all things (the who and the why of creation), while simultaneously leaving room for scientific inquiry into the processes and/or length of time God used to form creation (the when and the how).

A third area of diverse theological opinion has to do with the study of the last days or eschatology. Here Wesleyan traditions unswervingly affirm the belief that Christ will return again to redeem and judge all things. Wesleyans regularly leave open to discussion within the "big tent" of the church, however, the specific eschatological theories such as premillennialism, postmillennialism, or amillennialism. No single view is required.

In these various ways Wesleyan traditions have tried to keep unity of fellowship while allowing for differences of opinions. The hope is that the Wesleyan spirit will abide and allow unity on the essentials of faith while lovingly debating nonessentials. This aspect of the Wesleyan tradition seems more in tune with postmodern tendencies.

The term "generous orthodoxy," coined by Hans Frei, is often associated with postmodern voices. A generous orthodoxy has become a way of describing an emerging theological sensibility that tries to chart a path beyond often heated quarrels. Theologians like Stanley Grenz invite the church to "renew the center" in an attempt to avoid the polarizations of the past. Emerging church writer Brian McLaren hopes that the church will learn to balance orthodoxy with right living (orthopraxy) and a right heart (orthopathy), while not ignoring right thinking or right worship (orthodoxy).

Although "orthopraxy" and "orthopathy" were not terms Wesley used, they fit well with the spirit of his life and faith (Wesleyan traditions that are true to their heritage try to avoid the spirit of Ephesus that places doctrinal boundary keeping above holy love.)

John the apostle makes famously clear in his first Epistle that the demonstration that we are children of God is not that we believe the right set of propositions. It is that we embody the love of God in our relationships with one another. Those who know God will love, but those who do not know God do not love others (1 John 4).

Learning to have a "big tent" is not an easy task. It allows those who have not seen God, however, to recognize the divine love made manifest in our life together as the Body of Christ. And that sounds like good news to many postmodern ears.

qUESTIONS

1. What do you think about the "big tent" idea the author suggests?

2. Why do you think that Christians are tempted to maintain doctrinal purity at the risk of sacrificing love?

3. How might someone decide which aspects or ideas in the Christian's life are essential and which are not?

4. How can differences of opinion about the Bible undermine the move toward unity? What should be done?

5. What are orthodoxy, orthopraxy, and orthopathy? How are these related or different? Does it matter?

aPPLICATION

In light of this chapter and its topics, how might you act differently? Think differently? Feel differently? Relate differently?

tRUTH aND pOSTMODERNISM

tHOMAS jAY oORD

Postmodernists reject truth.

At least that's what many Christians think. Type "Christian," "truth," and "postmodern" into an Internet search engine, and you'll find plenty of Christian apologists saying that postmodernism abolishes truth.

These apologists typically react to postmodernism by declaring that God *is* truth. They quote the biblical passage saying that Jesus is the truth. Or they contrast postmodernism with Biblical Truth (capital letters required).

But does postmodernism require rejecting truth?

A wide variety of postmodern traditions exist. So answering this question well is difficult. In this chapter, we briefly explore some central issues regarding truth.

tHE lOSS oF cERTAINTY

The story of truth in the postmodern traditions begins with a modernist: René Descartes. Descartes discovered that our five senses—sight, smell, touch, taste, sound—cannot give absolute certain knowledge about the world.

We all make mistakes. These mistakes often occur because of faulty sense perception. We think we see water on the roadway, for instance, but it turns out to be an optical illusion. We think we hear our name being called, but our hearing is impaired. We think we're tasting beef, but it turns out to be deer. Our senses are not foolproof.

Descartes came to believe that we cannot know with absolute certainty the truth about objects beyond ourselves. Certainty cannot be attained through sense perception.

It's hard to overestimate the impact of this loss of absolute certainty about what we can know through our senses. So much of what we consider true comes from sensory perception. And yet we have to admit that our senses are not 100 percent accurate.

One modern response to Descartes is to say that language gives us a certain foundation for knowledge. We can be certain about verbal statements that are logically coherent with one another. Various statements—often called propositions—claim to mirror reality faithfully or describe reality fully.

Some Christians jump on the bandwagon that propositions provide absolute certainty. We can have absolute certainty about reality, they say, if the dogmatic propositions we affirm rest on a certain and sure foundation.

The foundation many modern Christians adopt is the Bible. They assume that God inspired the writing of the Bible in such a way as to produce it error-free. These Christians insist that biblical inerrancy and infallibility guarantee the Bible as a certain foundation for knowledge. Such a deduction defends Christianity from both infidels and modern critics.

Sadly, the modern project of biblical inerrancy collapses on itself. A close reading of the text reveals numerous inconsistencies. And the oldest manuscripts from which our Bibles come differ. Those who cling to the idea of an inerrant Bible must invent wild interpretations to reconcile these inconsistencies. Or they offer the worthless claim that the biblical autographs—which no longer exist—were inerrant. And when history, science, or literature contradicts the Bible, inerrantists are forced to reject this knowledge. They claim that the Bible is *the* book of all truth. It is the authority concerning not only all things religious but also all things economic, civic, historic, and scientific.

eXTREME rELATIVISM

If our perceptions about the world cannot provide us with absolute certainty, if language cannot give certainty, and if the Bible is not a certain foundation, on what basis can we speak of truth at all?

Extreme relativists—including some who adopt the label "postmodernist"—believe we cannot be confident that some statements about reality are truer than others. The truth of any statement—for example, the sun is hot—is ultimately up to the individual or is socially constructed. Extreme relativism says that truth is whatever any person or group decides.

Extreme relativism has many problems. These problems lead other postmodernists to reject the idea that truth is completely dependent upon the individual or the group.

The first problem is that extreme relativism is inconsistent with itself. After all, extreme relativism says it is true that there is no ultimate truth. And yet extreme relativists sound as if they intend this claim to be ultimately true even if some people choose not to believe it.

The second problem with extreme relativism, say some postmodernists, is that it cannot be consistently lived. We all presuppose that some statements about the world are truer than others. The way we live reveals this presupposition. Our friendships, our court system, our agricultural practices, our marriage arrangements, and so on, all presuppose that some views are truer than others. We don't have to know all truth to know this.

Finally, extreme relativism flies in the face of a number of central Christian claims about the superiority and enhanced value of living a life of love. Even if Christians cannot know reality in its fullness, the Christian message seems based upon the view that some ways of living are better than others. And some statements about reality are truer.

hUMILITY aND cONVICTION

Postmodern Christians can live faithfully between the absence of absolute certainty and the abyss of extreme relativism. This middle ground promotes both humility and conviction.

Postmodernists reject the idea that we can know with absolute certainty the full truth about reality. Absolute certainty requires inerrant sense perception. It requires a set of inerrant ideas. Or it requires an inerrant interpretation of an inerrant source. Such inerrancy does not exist.

This lack of absolute certainty about the full truth of reality, however, is not bad news for Christians. After all, *faith* resides at the heart of the Christian message. Christians are believers not proposition defenders.

Faith is different from absolute certainty. But it's different from absolute mystery too. Faith need not be blind or unreasonable.

To believe is not to reject reason or evidence altogether. One can affirm a degree of confidence in the greater plausibility of statements, ways of living, or perceptions. And this greater confidence can foster reasonable conviction. Faith can be grounded.

A number of postmodernists affirm that what we regard as true extends well beyond verbal statements. Truth also has a livable, embodied element. It has an aesthetic element too. Truth is personal, communal, and even cosmic. Truth is multifaceted.

Postmodernists recognize that we cannot comprehend truth entirely. We see through a glass darkly. And this inability to be absolutely certain or to know reality fully should lead us to humility.

Pride still comes before a fall. But pride emerges not only when we retain full control of our lives but also when we think we have full and certain knowledge. We forget that the just live by faith. Postmodernism can foster the virtue of humble living.

In sum, postmodernists need not reject truth. But postmodernism reminds us that "we know in part." Christian convictions embraced in humility can help us live an abundant life in our emerging world.

qUESTIONS

1. Do you feel threatened or encouraged about this chapter? Why?

2. How do we know things are true? What is the difference in believing the sun gives off heat and that God loves the world?

3. Can there be a relationship between faith and absolute certainty? Why or why not?

4. Is evidenceless or reason-free faith enough for us Christians or should we search for evidence, reasons, and even proofs for our beliefs?

5. How do you feel about rejecting both extreme relativism and absolute certainty?

aPPLICATION

In light of this chapter and its topics, how might you act differently? Think differently? Feel differently? Relate differently?

tHE cHURCH aND pOSTMODERN pOP cULTURE

jOSEPH bANKARD

As a professor of philosophy at a Christian liberal arts university, I often supplement course material with movie clips, novels, goofy videos found on YouTube, and an occasional piece of music. My students usually pay special attention to what I am trying to teach when I use these supplementary materials from popular culture.

Recently, I showed an especially provocative movie to my classes for extra credit. Fifteen minutes into the film a student stood up abruptly and walked out of the classroom. The next day, I received a very polite e-mail from this student asking, among other things, why a professor would show such a movie at a Christian university.

This question is an important one. It not only represents a basic sentiment shared by many Christians—especially those raised in Holiness traditions—but also captures the focus of this essay. Why would a Christian professor use media present in popular culture, such as movies, music, novels, and art? Is there any justification to use popular media given the warnings found in scriptures such as Col. 3:2-5? That passage reads, "Set your minds on things that are above, not on things that are on earth, for you have died, and your life is hidden with Christ in God. . . . Put to death, therefore, whatever in you is earthly: fornication, impurity, passion, evil desire, and greed" (NRSV).

In my e-mail response to the disgruntled student, I pointed out all of the redeeming qualities in the provocative film (I argued that the movie in question was about the beauty of brokenness, the importance of authenticity, and the need for acceptance and love. Given these themes, it seemed reasonable to show such a film to Christian students who also cherish these kinds of themes.)

The concern expressed by this one student reveals a larger tension surrounding the relationship between the Christian church and popular culture more generally. This essay is an attempt to address some of these questions directly. I want to highlight two fundamental problems the church sometimes makes in its general disposition toward popular culture. And I want to provide a third position that is more Wesleyan and more compatible with the rising popularity of postmodern philosophy.

(The first and most common mistake the church makes in its relationship with pop culture is to reject it categorically, while using the artificial categories "secular" and "sacred." These categories are artificial because they don't refer to anything real. Outside of God, is there anything we would consider *fully* sacred? Similarly, if God's redemptive work extends beyond the boundaries of the Christian church, should we label anything *completely* secular? How can anything be inherently secular if an omnipresent God is present to it in some way?

(The line separating what is secular from what is sacred becomes blurred when we take a close look at our world. Most, if not all, actually existing things or people contain elements of both. Of course, some things, events, or people better reflect what is godly than others. But an absolute distinction between what is secular and what is sacred doesn't accurately depict the world we experience.)

Because of this, I don't think the church should be in the business of labeling things as entirely holy or absolutely unholy. Instead, I think the church should foster meaningful spaces throughout God's creation, regardless of where it finds them (God is present everywhere, and God's will may be finding fulfillment in some surprising places.)

(One of the important doctrines in the Wesleyan tradition is called prevenient grace. This doctrine suggests that God acts first and engages *all* people, creatures, and creation. If we really take prevenient grace seriously, we must acknowledge the possibility that the creative, dynamic, and loving work of God might be revealed in unexpected ways and places. After all, there should be no limits placed on God's redemptive reach.)

The conviction that God works in people and places outside the boundaries of the church makes it possible for me to watch popular movies, listen to popular music, or read a popular novel without missing the moments when God's love and compassion break through. God is present in and can be revealed through all sorts of media. And because God is present, all forms of media might reveal something true, lovely, beautiful, compassionate, or authentic.

The second mistake the church can make is to surrender its prophetic voice for the sake of tolerance or cultural relevance. We must remember that the biblical prophets pointed out the ways in which believers should act as a divinely called people.

There is a difference between, on one hand, the general virtues of love, compassion, authenticity, and forgiveness and, on the other, God's radical call to the church. This radical call can be lost when Christian discipleship is reduced to some vague notion of kindness. (It is a mistake to limit God's work to the confines of the church) But it is also a mistake to equate Christianity to some set of general virtues. The church should affirm all of the ways God is working in the world, while maintaining the unique call God places on the church.

(All people—whether Muslim, Jew, Buddhist, or atheist—are potentially capable of love, forgiveness, and compassion. And to the degree each person chooses to act virtuously, that person participates in God's salvific work.)

However, there are important differences between a kind atheist and a kind Christian. The atheist may sometimes respond appropriately to God's general will as a result of prevenient grace. But the Christian is a member of the Christian community that is grounded in God's particular revelation. And God's call to the

Christian will likely include but go beyond the general call for kindness that God, through prevenient grace, extends to the atheist.

In a similar way, popular media may provide moments of inspiration, beauty, and love without being rightfully labeled "Christian." Being Christian means something very specific, and the church must profess this particularity.

In sum, the proper relationship between the Christian church and popular culture allows for God's revelation to extend to media such as music, novels, art, and film. Yet the Christian church maintains a unique call and place in God's story. Understanding that God acts everywhere through prevenient grace but also extends a particular call to the church may be central to helping Christians understand how to engage postmodern culture well.

qUESTIONS

1. Do you see the labels "secular" and "sacred" still at work within the Church? Are those labels used outside the Church? Are these labels helpful? Why or why not?

2. Do you feel something is being lost or gained by blurring the distinction between the "secular" and "sacred"? Does this blurring make you hopeful or nervous? Why?

3. What is this chapter offering the Church?

4. What is at stake in this chapter? Is it something bigger than simply giving Christians permission to enjoy popular books, movies, and music?

5. This essay suggests that non-Christians can demonstrate some of the same virtues that Jesus asked his followers to demonstrate. Do you agree with this? What does it mean?

aPPLICATION

In light of this chapter and its topics, how might you act differently? Think differently? Feel differently? Relate differently?

5 gENDER, eTHNICITY, aND eCONOMICS

dEIRDRE bROWER lATZ

For a long time, we have known that humans differ from each other. Today, we seem to be confronted more directly by these differences than ever before. In our neighborhoods, our churches, on television, or on the Internet, we interact with people who are sometimes very different from us. Often difference in the Church has been considered a breach of unity. Yet difference is central to our postmodern world.

What does difference mean for us today? Does it really matter that we differ from one another in gender, economic status, and ethnicity? And given these differences, can Christians truly be different from each other and yet worship God in unity?

Fortunately, these questions are not entirely new. If we look at the New Testament, we see examples of people wrestling with questions of how the Holy Spirit can empower oneness in the midst of difference. We wrestle today with similar questions.

I think that the predominant impulse of the church should be radical egalitarianism. In other words, the church should be wary of setting up structures that consider some people as essentially better than others. At its best, the Church has rejected the idea that people are better or worse based on gender, economic status, or race.

Postmodernism makes us more aware of the inequalities that have been imposed upon people whose gender, economic status, and ethnicity were not considered best. And postmodernism enables the Church to ask about the degree to which the Church has been helpful or hurtful in the fostering of these differences.

Some postmodern Christians say that the Church needs to embody faithful storytelling as a way to proclaim the story of the gospel in this postmodern age. Jesus said that the gospel should be good news to poor people. "Poor people" refers not only to the economically disadvantaged but also to those who are socially marginalized and excluded.

If the Church takes seriously what it means to bring good news to poor people, multiple changes—conversions—will be needed. Only through multiple conversions can the Church be one storytelling community that engages contemporary culture(s). The open dialogue between Christianity and postmodernity I envision would, in fact, include several of the following conversions.

Postmodernism calls Christians to convert from *individualism* to a revalued *life-in-community*. This includes understanding the contributions of both women and men as crucial. We are not a collection of individuals. We are baptized into the one Body of Christ, and we are members of one another.

Christians need to convert from us-and-them to thinking them-as-us. Usually *they* are over there, out there, and above all, not in here. The unity of them-as-us means that we value others more than ourselves. Differing voices, genders, ethnicities, bank balances, opinions, ways of being, and practices can enable the church to embody the diversity of the Triune God.

(John Wesley is a good example for us, because he resisted the urge to make poor people "objects" in quite this way. Instead, he believed knowing personally people who are poor was vital to the healthy Christian life.)

(Shared conversation, shared space, learning each other's names and stories, and discovering economic differences should not become barriers to being one in Christ. They only become barriers when the church does not practice what it preaches)

(Postmodernism calls Christians to convert from monologue proclamations to dialogue conversations. This means moving from being primarily speechmakers to becoming conversation partners. We—the church—must become good listeners.

Jesus can make us feel uncomfortable when we discover that sitting and talking with "the sinner" is woven into the story of the gospel. Being part of a rainbow people means crossing cultures as a part of cross-shaped living.

Christians must also convert from being oriented toward consumption to being oriented toward generosity. Can we really say we love our brothers and sisters in Christ while they go hungry, are naked, become sick, or are lonely in prison?

The question of our relationship with money will be a constant test as we seek unity. It is hard to know a woman's name, play with her children, and take Communion alongside her, all the while knowing that she goes hungry at night. And postmodernism pushes us to ask about the economic and social structures that oppress hungry people.

Postmodernism also calls Christians to convert from political apathy to prophetic imagination. A prophetic imagination dreams about what might be, by God's grace. In part, this means aligning ourselves with practices of unity. This might entail sharing goods, community living, and consuming less.

With a prophetic imagination, the church might become a community in which men and women pour their lives out for one another, respect one another's differences, swap stories, and share lives.

Of course, life in an egalitarian community cannot emerge without some conflict. Just as in any family, we will need to forgive one another, stretch one another's thinking, and challenge one another's practices. Insofar as we are different, we take the risk of loving across boundaries.

Finally, postmodernism calls Christians to convert from monochrome to multicolored. Our worship might become an occasion of cross-cultural hospitality. We might demonstrate—in practice—the reconciling power of God in the gritty and sometimes messy reality of worship preferences that are quite diverse. We do so, believing that those whose preferences differ from ours are nonetheless our brothers and sisters. We share and break bread with them.

(So what difference do ethnicity, gender, and economic differences make? In one way, none. After all, radical equality, generous love, and knowing one another deeply are the reality of the gospel.) In another way, postmodernism helps us question the roots of inequality. It has helped us renew conversations about hospitality and humility. Postmodernism alerts us to the ways that oppression has been prevalent in institutions, including the church.

We Wesleyans need to recognize all of this. And where needed, we must repent, convert, and become a voice of restoration, hope, radical equality, and gracious generosity. The Church is beautiful and fashioned by God in its diversity, and this is a hallmark of its unity. For in knowing and loving those who are other—regardless of ethnicity, gender, and economics—we can be one body.

qUESTIONS

1. Have you seen the church working against economic, gender, and racial oppression or fostering it?

2. Why are we so quick to consider others as "other" in our world? What are some steps toward becoming a church that attempts to see people not as "other"?

3. Why is it hard to love persons who are so very different? What is the threat?

4. What about this move from consumption to generosity? What does that look like in our homes? What might that look like in our churches and places of work?

aPPLICATION

In light of this chapter and its topics, how might you act differently? Think differently? Feel differently? Relate differently?

6 tYPES oF pOSTMODERNISM

tHOMAS jAY oORD

Postmodernism. Some love it. Some hate it.

What it means to be postmodern usually depends on the one speaking. And people often talk about *the* postmodern way of looking at some issue. In fact, an assortment of postmodernisms exists.

For some, postmodernism teems with possibility. It invites us to go beyond what presses, depresses, or oppresses, breaking from negative precedent while reclaiming what is good from the past.

But postmodernism is also misused, abused, and overused. Almost everything new gets labeled postmodern, at least temporarily.

Four overarching ways of talking about postmodernism have emerged in recent years. These four traditions share at least one thing in common: they seek to go beyond what each deems modern.

We can avoid confusion if we remember that "modern" and "now" are not synonymous. Modernity refers to ways of living, ideas and beliefs, or paradigms. The deep-seated intuition that change is in the air—felt by peoples of diverse visions and convictions—stimulates interest in postmodernism.

The remainder of this chapter very briefly describes four postmodernisms.

tHE pROBLEM wITH wORDS: dECONSTRUCTIVE pOSTMODERNISM

Deconstructive postmodernism identifies inconsistencies in the language we use to describe the world. Modernists base their knowledge about the world upon language and universal reason. They think that language offers a certain, secure, and unambiguous foundation for understanding reality. Modernists assume that words capture truth fully.

Deconstructive postmodernism notes, however, that words inevitably contain unintended meanings. Even our most cherished words—"God," "love," "world," "Jesus," "hope"—are ambiguous. People disagree about the full meaning of these words. Language never offers a sure foundation.

Fans of deconstructive postmodernism point out that it affirms diversity and variety. It does not idolize words, and it demands humility. Deconstruction rejects traditional hierarchies that keep many at the margins of society. This postmodernism calls attention to the "other."

Critics argue that deconstructionism implies that each individual alone determines truth. Radical relativism reigns. Deconstructive postmodernism provides no basis for ultimate meaning.

Critics also say that deconstructive postmodernism is self-refuting. It relies on ambiguous words to maintain that language is ambiguous. Critics suggest that deconstructionists look for a deeper source than language to establish their claims.

a sTORY tO oRIENT oUR lIVES: nARRATIVE pOSTMODERNISM

Narrative postmodernism claims that meaning and truth are found in stories. The stories we tell and the way we tell them arise from particular points of view. And our particular points of view are only intelligible as part of a community's story.

Narrative postmodernism believes that understanding reality as story overcomes two problems central to modernism. One is the modern claim that logic, mathematics, and the natural sciences offer the only adequate bricks for building a meaningful worldview. When playing by the rules of modernity, theology becomes gibberish.

The second problem, say narrative postmodernists, is that each individual alone decides what is true or meaningful. Truth is individualistic, and individualism is modernity's calling card.

Narrative postmodernism argues that meaning is found in, and arises out of, communities. Truth is communal. Truth is lived, not primarily contemplated. This means that conversion is more about joining a community than embracing a new set of beliefs.

Narrative postmodernism in its Christian form retrieves beliefs and practices that modernity's rationalistic and individualistic biases discarded. Narrative postmodernists view the Bible as offering stories arising from particular forms of life. The Bible offers a message to be lived, not statements to be analytically defended.

Narrative postmodernism has its critics, of course. Critics argue that it allows no genuine criticism from within the community. No one can question the old, old story. Narrative postmodernism has a difficulty challenging community practices and ideologies that promote patriarchy, anti-Semitism, or ecological recklessness.

Critics also worry that this postmodernism tradition offers no universal standards by which to assess beliefs "outside" the communities. God's omnipresent voice may be speaking through those outside Christendom.

bREAKING fREE:
lIBERATIONIST pOSTMODERNISM

Liberationist postmodernism argues that modern ideas, beliefs, and ways of living are oppressive. Liberationists want freedom to live a better life.

Feminist postmodernism claims that modern (and premodern) worldviews regard males as superior. Common language and customs perpetuate, often unintentionally, the idea that women are inferior. Postmodern feminists call upon contemporary people to speak and live in ways that empower women.

Ethnic postmodernism champions issues of culture and race. Modernity considers everyone fundamentally the same. Ethnic postmodernists argue, by contrast, that cultural uniqueness should be valued. Persons of color are oppressed when white is considered right.

Ecological postmodernism places the issues of environmental well-being at the fore of contemporary attention. Modernity considered the world a machine and its creatures in need of domination. Ecological postmodernists argue that the world and its creatures are not well understood in mechanistic terms. All creatures are intrinsically valuable.

Liberation postmodernism has theological implications. Postmodern feminists argue that modernity's masculine God fails to affirm experiences typically identified with females. But God is not male. Ethnic postmodernists argue that minorities have been conquered and slaughtered in the name of modernity's God. But God is not white. Ecological postmodernists believe that the earth has been raped and debilitated by humans who believed that God commanded them to subdue nonhumans. God is green.

Opponents of liberationist postmodernism typically claim that these criticisms are too severe. Theology at its best never regards God as male, white, or concerned only with humans. Critics also worry that liberationist postmodernism adopts deconstruction. Deconstructionism offers no constructive basis for the freedom that liberationists desperately desire.

rECLAIMING tO mOVE aHEAD: rEVISIONARY pOSTMODERNISM

Revisionary postmodernism identifies the nonnegotiables of life, draws from past wisdom, and incorporates novel ideas to propose a credible worldview.

Revisionary postmodernists accept the project of reconstructing a vision of reality. They seek a story big and adequate enough to include everyone. And yet this grand story promotes diversity and difference.

Revisionary postmodernism argues that our experience is prior to and more basic than language. Beliefs that we inevitably presuppose in experience should be privileged. They are experiential nonnegotiables. They help us avoid radical relativism.

While modernism said that knowledge came only by what we perceive through our five senses, revisionary postmodernism says that we know in other ways. For instance, the Holy Spirit can be directly experienced despite not being perceptible through our five senses.

Revisionists join narrative postmodernists in looking to ancient sources for wisdom. But they also embrace emergent insights that help us live an abundant life.

Critics of revisionary postmodernism are typically worried about one of three things. Some regard worldview construction as inherently oppressive. Some Christian critics believe that revisionists do not retrieve enough from premodern Christendom. And some critics object to this postmodernism's relational God.

cONCLUSION

Which postmodernism best informs or supplements the Wesleyan tradition? Does any postmodernism undermine Wesleyan ways? These are questions for us to address in this increasingly postmodern age.

qUESTIONS

1. What is your first reaction to hearing the word "postmodern"? Why do you think you have that reaction?

2. What do you think are the strengths and weaknesses of believing that words are at least partly ambiguous?

3. What grand stories have shaped the way you think about life?

4. What kinds of liberation do you think are most needed in today's world?

5. What do you think about the idea that we should seek a story big enough to include everyone?

aPPLICATION

In light of this chapter and its topics, how might you act differently? Think differently? Feel differently? Relate differently?

cRITICAL rESPONSE— pOSTMODERNISM

gERARD rEED

George Orwell, writing (in 1949) his classic dystopia, *1984*, envisioned a time when "All words grouping themselves round the concepts of objectivity and rationalism were contained in the single word *oldthink*."[1] Thus Orwell prophetically warned against the twin pillars of postmodernism: epistemological skepticism and ethical relativism. We cannot know "truth" regarding objective reality, the Postmodernists say, so we "construct" it in either individual or social ways; we cannot know what's universally right and wrong, so we determine, on a subjective level, how we or our group choose to behave. Concurrently with Orwell, Arnold J. Toynbee was writing his massive *A Study of History*, and with an entirely different frame of reference he concluded that Western civilization had begun to decline primarily because it had embraced irrationality and relativism.[2] In short, growing numbers of people were living out the title of Luigi Pirandello's 1916 play, *Right You Are If You Think You Are*.

What Orwell called oldthink (objective reason), postmodernists reject and claim to transcend. Thus Professor Oord rightly describes some of the dominant currents within this cultural movement. Some "deconstructive" postmodernists, following Jacques Derrida and Michel Foucault, seek to get behind or beneath the apparent meaning of language. More deeply, following the atheistic and nihilistic approach of Friedrich Nietzsche, they deconstruct not only language but reality itself! Nothing can be said because, ultimately, nothing ontological is really *there*. If there are objective "things" (and especially all eternal, substantial, nonmaterial realities) around us—they are beyond knowing and thus unreal.(What's real is simply what, at the moment, we consider real for us, whatever works for us.)

Narrative postmodernists, as Oord notes, find meaning in stories. There are, consequently, many links between postmodernism and the modern media—films and TV construct an imaginary world wherein viewers detach themselves from any objective reality. But nothing need be *true* in the stories (whether historical, biblical, or literary). What matters, say some literary critics, is the "reader's response." What's important is what I *feel* when reading or hearing or seeing the story. When a story speaks to me (or to my particular group) I find momentary clarity or contentment.

Liberationist postmodernists identify with an oppressed group and demand that their "truth" be granted simply because they entertain it, and all groups (whether Aztecs or Athenians, Stalinists or Jihadists) have a right to their "opinions." Thus feminists such as Peggy McIntosh insist that women think differently from men—"laterally," privileging relationships more than "facts" or "objective norms."[3] And if women see different "truths" in physics or ethics, for example, no one can say they are wrong, for there are equally worthy "different" ways of thinking.

"Revisionary postmodernism" seems to garner Professor Oord's approbation. Intent on "reconstructing a vision of reality," they accept the deconstructionists' skepticism regarding reality's knowability. But in fact, while they may want to retain some of the wisdom of the past and grant some validity to objective truths, their governing assumptions render their aspiration utopian—a subjectively reconstructed "story big and adequate enough to include everyone."

In addition to describing postmodernism, Professor Oord proposes it as a possible position for Wesleyans. To do so he first accepts René Descartes's famous critique of sense knowledge. What Professor Oord fails to note is that the overwhelming majority of great philosophers (including Plato, Aristotle, Augustine, Aquinas, and C. S. Lewis) have been metaphysical *realists*, relying upon the information supplied by the senses, as corrected by our reason, to think in accord with a "correspondence theory of truth." As Aristotle said, in his *Metaphysics*, "To say of what is that it is and of ▬ what is not that it is not, is true." As expanded upon by his Christian follower, Thomas Aquinas said, "All existing things, namely, all real objects outside the soul, possess something intrinsic that allows us to call them true" (QDV 1.5.2). Consequently: "In created things there is truth on two levels: in the things themselves and in the perceiving mind" (QDV 1.6).[4]

Seeing a deer leads me to study, in a biology class, the genetic structure that establishes its form—the same form that enables me to differentiate a deer from a grizzly bear in the forest, a quite *real* distinction that has *absolute* bearing on my survival! Studying history I see free moral agents whose actions have shaped past events—and I discern intrinsic traits (such as original sin) that typify human beings. Certainly, as Descartes said, my senses occasionally mislead me. But just as "hard cases make poor law," so too a few misleading sense impressions never prompt me to deny their general accuracy. Though a mirage looks like water on the horizon, anyone who has seen a few of them learns to dismiss it as an illusion. To disregard our unique ability to know trustworthy truths about the world would brush aside all the amazingly accurate scientific work so basic to human history.

To a philosophical realist, "truth" rightly aligns the mind with what is real. We live in an objectively real world, a world other-than-us. When we discern "truth," our minds conform to what is. So I say, without hesitation, that there are mountains in Colorado, that there was an American Civil War, that I am a retired professor, and so on. Realists also take as intuitively certain the basic laws of logic—identity and noncontradiction and excluded middle—and insist they apply everywhere to everyone. Still more: ▬ there are moral laws written into the very fabric of our being by the source of all moral truth—Being Itself—that we can rationally discern. With Paul, realists see a "law written in their hearts, their conscience also bearing witness" (Rom. 2:15, NKJV) to imperatives such as "do no wrong," "do not murder," "do not steal," and so on.

(Postmodernists often dismiss not only universal moral laws and the laws of logic but also propositional truths such as those found in biblical revelation.)(Note, incidentally, that both Professor Oord and I rely almost entirely on declarative, or indicative, sentences—propositional statements, making *absolute* truth claims. We assume the words we write *correspond* to some reality that you, the reader, can also know as you think the same words.) Accordingly, orthodox Christians, both Catholic and Protestant, have ever insisted that the Bible reveals, in propositional language, certain divinely inspired truths regarding God and humanity.

To question the infallibility of the Scriptures (as do antifoundational postmodernists by doubting their "inerrancy") leaves one without the major source of authoritative truth for orthodox Christians. Consider, as representative, the recent (1965) declaration of the Second Vatican Council of the Roman Catholic Church, the "Dogmatic Constitution on Divine Revelation," which decrees that "in His goodness and wisdom, God chose to reveal Himself and to make known to us the hidden purpose of His will." He established a redemptive plan, running from Genesis to Revelation, and

> This plan of revelation is realized by deeds and words having an inner unity: the deeds wrought by God in the history of salvation manifest and confirm the teaching and realities signified by the words, while the words proclaim the deeds and clarify the mystery contained in them. By this revelation then, the deepest truth about God and the salvation of man is made clear to us in Christ who is the Mediator at the same time the fullness of all revelation (1.2).

Consequently,

> It follows that the books of Scripture must be acknowledged as teaching firmly, faithfully, and without error that truth which God wanted to put into the sacred writings for the sake of our salvation. Therefore "all Scripture is inspired by God and useful for teaching, for reproving, for correcting, for instruction in justice; that the man of God may be perfect, equipped for every good work (2 Tim. 3:16-17, Greek text)" (3.11).[5]

Inasmuch as postmodernism rejects both the realist's correspondence theory of truth and the traditional Christian commitment to biblical revelation, it offers little for believers who want to trust in anything more than inner affirmations and consolations.

In rejecting "extreme relativism," Professor Oord distances himself from many of the most prominent and influential postmodernists, such as Derrida and Foucault, who are anything but humble and tolerant in their dogmatic insistence on skepticism and relativism. Yet he thinks there is an admirable humility in the refusal to make strong truth claims. And he values a tentative confidence in a faith that dares to trust both a God and His Word that cannot be clearly, certainly known.

While much may be learned from postmodernism, Christians committed to the proposition that "in the beginning was the Word, and the Word was with God, and the Word was God," and "all things were made through Him, and without Him nothing was made that was made" (John 1:1, 3, NKJV) cannot but reject its central tenets.

qUESTION

What do you find helpful or unhelpful in this critical response?

cONVERSATION iGNITER
mri mIRACLES

lEONARD sWEET

* * *

"My times are in your hand."
—Ps. 31:15 (NRSV)

* * *

My brother, Phil, is a professor and chair of the language department at Radford University, one of the University of Virginia schools. The only person I know who is intellectually more gifted is my other brother John. But Phil's genius does not prevent him from being somewhat of a troglodyte, a neo-Luddite to be more precise. Phil is comfortable living in the world his beloved Johannes Gutenberg built, and he only moves slowly into a Google world, kicking and screaming as he goes. (We say Gutenberg, but really the Chinese got to the printing press first: the first book printed, dated, was in 868 in China).

For the past couple of years Phil's youngest son has served in the Peace Corps in Senegal. Nikolas lives in the middle of Kedougou village in a thatched hut, and he keeps his "Uncle Len" informed of his welfare by copying me when he sends e-mail updates to family and friends. I have kept all of my nephew's communications, but two in particular have been especially joyous in the way they tweaked and teased his "genius" father.

In one e-mail, Nikolas kidded his father that he probably had a higher bandwidth access from his thatched cottage than his father enjoyed while sitting in his university office. In my other favorite e-mail, Nikolas attached a couple of pictures of village life in Kedougou. Bicycles were everywhere, and everyone on a bicycle seemed to be talking on a cell phone. There was even one picture of a Sengalese driving a goat-cart while talking on his cell phone.

A case could be made for these two technologies, the bicycle and the cell phone, as the major shapers of the world this book is calling "postmodern." For both technologies, the bicycle and the cell phone, changed everything. Studies of both church records and marriage registers reveal that the introduction of the bicycle enabled people to choose which church in which village they would attend and to find a mate outside the parish in which they were born. In fact, one historian makes the case that the Middle Ages and its traditional understandings of community didn't end in many country villages until the invention of the bicycle, and especially its more widespread introduction in the 1890s with the use of the chain drive and pneumatic tires, and the addition of three-speed gears and gas lamps in the 1900s.[1]

Within 35 years after Martin Cooper's first cell-phone call in 1973, over half the world's population (3.3 billion) boasted cell phones. Not only did this represent the fastest diffusion of any technology in history, it also meant that over half the world's population are connected to one another and to the wisdom of the ages. One of the most magical destinations in my earliest memory was the Gloversville Public Library, one of the 1700 "free libraries" built by Andrew Carnegie over a thirty year period on the belief that the throbbing heart of any thriving community needed to be a "free public library." When my brothers and I crossed the arched threshold of this library, an emporium of beauty and truth awaited us with spiral staircases, Gothic bookcases, and magic carpet rides to every place on the planet. Since 85 percent of all cell phones today come with Web access, every person with a cell phone now has a personal Carnegie Library. Or more accurately, a personal Stanford Library, Oxford Library and soon Library of Congress, since Google is scanning in all 8 million books in Stanford's collection, and Oxford has agreed to let Google scan anything printed before 1900, and the Library of Congress is starting a digital archive of at least one million books.

In short, another way of talking about this "postmodern shift" is to start with the realization that most of us reading these words are immigrants in the world we now experience. I am a native Gutenberger. I find myself now an immigrant in a Google world, with Googley children. I have glommed on to the words Matthew Arnold wrote on his honeymoon (presumably not about his honeymoon, though you would think he had better things to do), describing this "inbetweenness:"

Wandering between two worlds, one dead,
The other powerless to be born,
With nowhere yet to rest my head,
Like these, on earth I wait forlorn.
Their faith, my tears, the world deride;
I come to shed them at their side.[2]

I am starting to shy away from using the "postmodern" word, and frankly find this distinction between a Gutenberg World and a Google world more fertile for creative, constructive thought than the "modern" vs. "postmodern" language. First of all, there are so many people with pomo-phobia out there that they shut down or raise their dukes at the first mention of the word. Second, the word "postmodern" has come to be one of those vacuum words where everyone who uses it—from architects to philosophers to literary critics—sucks different meaning out of the concept until nothing is left.[3] One scholar, Ziony Zevit, humorously calls postmodernism "a refined, intellectual celebration of mindful anarchy conducted paradoxically by scholars in hierarchically organized elitist institutions of higher learning."[4] Third, I am open to using any language that will help the church stop imitating those beleaguered Japanese soldiers found in the mountains fighting the Second World War long after it ended.

If we are to take seriously the Wesley hymn that calls us "To Serve This Present [read 'Google'] Age, Our Calling to Fulfill," here are four questions that every church and every Christian should ask. The first is from Lyle Schaller (who started every church consultation with this five-word question), the second from Charles C. West, the third is from me, and the last is from St. Jerome, written 15 centuries ago.

(1) "What year is it here?"

(2) "We turn to God for help when our foundations are shaking, only to learn that it is God who is shaking them." There is a lot of shaking going on in our world today. To what extent is God "up to something" in the shaking of the world's foundations?

(3) Is your church incarnating the gospel in a Google mission field? Or are you expecting Googleys to give up their native culture and become Gutenbergers before they can be a part of your community?

(4) How relevant is St. Jerome's critique of the church of the 5th century?

Shame on us, the world is falling in ruins, but our sins still flourish. The glorious city that was the head of the Roman Empire has been engulfed in one terrific blaze. There is no part of the earth where exiles from Rome are not to be found. Churches once held sacred have fallen into dust and ashes, and still we set out hearts greedily on money. We live as though we were doomed to death on the morrow, but we build houses as though we were going to live for ever in this world. Our walls glitter with gold, gold gleams upon our ceilings and upon the capitals of our pillars; yet Christ is dying at our doors in the persons of the poor, naked and hungry . . . Flocks and shepherds perish together, because the priest is now even as the people.[5]

Possible paper Topic !

pART II
tHE gOSPEL iN pOSTMODERNITY

tHE tRUSTWORTHINESS aND aUTHORITY oF tHE bIBLE

kARA j. lYONS-pARDUE

Context is important for any worldview that calls itself postmodern. Some people think the slogan "That's true for you, but not for me" sums up the postmodern outlook. Although it is a stereotype, this kind of relativism does exist in some postmodernism traditions. And this raises a problem for the role of the Bible: if truth depends on our individual contexts, how can one book possibly be universally truthful or authoritative?

The truth is, postmodernism poses questions that, for much of its history, Christianity was not pressed to answer: "What makes Scripture true?" "Is the Bible reliable?" "Why do I have to believe in Jesus if it does not work for me?" "What makes this book more reliable than the Qur'an or the Vedas?"

(When taken seriously, these questions push Christian conversations into uncomfortable and even gray areas. But we will understand the Bible better if we hear what postmodernists are asking and recognize the difference context makes.)

Postmodernism calls into question the pat answers to life's questions that end in "because the Bible tells me so." Even good people have heated debates over biblical meanings. (This Good Book can be misused by evil people to support sinful deeds. Biblical texts were used, for instance, in support of both sides of the American slavery debate. And biblical prophecies have been the basis of many past predictions of the world's imminent end. Yet we are still here, still reading, and still disagreeing.)

A Wesleyan perspective on Scripture pushes Christians to let the minor disagreements slide and focus in on what is central to faith. This requires interpretation. Texts alone do not produce meaning. They require someone to read and reflect on them so that they have life.

But a reader's context can cause a lot of varying interpretations. Our experience is an inescapable lens through which we approach the Bible. And while a reader's context is important, Scripture already presents us with a web of contexts that influence our reading.

If I wanted to grow a garden, I would not seek instruction in a biology textbook, even though the science behind photosynthesis would certainly be helpful. Why not? Books are written for different purposes. Part of being a responsible reader is the ability to discern these literary differences, whether by genre (e.g., poem, history, letter) or by purpose (e.g., theological, instructional, memoir).)

As Protestants, we tend to think of the Bible as "a book." But it is really two volumes totaling sixty-six books in all. Just as the volumes vary in size, the books are vastly different lengths.

Even the names of our testaments push us to recognize their contextual relationship to one another. The Old Testament is not "old," as in obsolete or outdated. But it is so named because it is "older" than its newer biblical counterpart. The New Testament is not entirely original either. It reiterates and continues the story that began in the first volume of God's story, the Old Testament. Postmodernism prods us to remember this context when we read from either testament.

Not all biblical books are created equal. Anyone who doubts this probably has not read 3 John or Numbers recently. Nonetheless, Christians believe that the Holy Spirit guided the writing and use of these books so that the final list of biblical books would continue to nourish the Church. This same Spirit guides our reading of Scripture today.

Still, the book's context matters. When we read poetry from the Psalms, for instance, that poetry expresses a person's anguish poured out before a gracious God. And we must recognize that a psalm serves a different purpose than a gospel story about Jesus' teaching to his disciples. They are both "true," but they reveal different things.

When Paul instructs the Corinthian Christians about Jesus' resurrection in 1 Corinthians 15, his teaching is foundational for the Christian hope in God's ultimate victory over death. When in Ecclesiastes 1 the wise man laments that everything under the sun is meaningless, we recognize that he is expressing justifiable human sorrow in a particular situation.

Postmodernism pushes us to recognize contextual differences like these. Saying that the whole Bible is "true" can easily miss the point. We must also ask, What is it good for? What *kind* of truth does it reveal?

Sometimes, scriptures contradict one another. In those instances, we should also look at the immediate context of the passages. When we come to particularly problematic verses, we must remember that there are verses before and after that set these isolated statements in context. And there are chapters and books of context to be examined.

Reading for context reminds us that we do not come to Scripture to strip-mine isolated truth claims and leave the majority of the text behind. We should soak in the stories, poems, and beautiful images. In so doing, these texts can form the very context through which we view the world.

Our most vital context as readers of Scripture is the Church: the community of faith. The Bible was never intended to be a one-person instruction manual. Many authors and many communities birthed these books, and we believe they were bathed in the Spirit's inspiration. We, too, are called to read, pray, debate, and sing these texts in the context of a believing community and open to the Spirit's inspiration.

When we talk about the varying contexts of the reader, things get even more complex. I am a white woman in North America. I bring a different context to my reading of Scripture than the man in church next to me. Even more so, an illiterate woman in rural Peru might hear a different message when the Bible is read aloud in her church.

Many contexts are morally neutral—being one gender or the other, being old or young. But other contexts blind us to our biases and lead us to excuse our sinfulness. Throughout Scripture, there is a persistent concern for the poor, the disenfranchised, and the powerless: widows, children, and the oppressed. If, instead, we use Scripture to defend the status quo and to excuse our desire for power, we are out of tune with the Bible's pulse of sacrificial love. Our context and motivations blind us.

The Bible does not function best as an absolute "trump card" to settle arguments. And postmodernism's emphasis on context reminds us that the Bible's truths are not universally accepted. We need not apologize that the Bible includes us in a specific story that asks specific—and even strange—things from believers.

Postmodernism gives a name to the risk we take in believing something particular. In trusting that the Bible truthfully reveals God's plan for salvation in Jesus Christ, mediated by the Spirit's presence in the Church, we are staking a claim. Our lives are test cases or "experiments" to demonstrate our Christian hypothesis that Jesus is the way, truth, and life. This requires faith, but not in the scientific accuracy or statistical reliability of the Bible. It requires faith in the God we encounter in the Bible.

qUESTIONS

1. What kind of questions have you heard raised about the Bible that Christians may not have been asked to answer in the past?

2. The author says that the Bible does not function best as an absolute trump card to settle arguments. What does this mean? Why might this be important?

3. How can the community of faith save us from looking at the Bible as a "one-person instruction manual"?

4. What does the writer mean by her statement that saying that the whole Bible is "true" can easily miss the point?

She says that we should actually ask what *kind* of truth the Bible reveals. And what is the Bible good for? Why might these last two questions be more important?

aPPLICATION

In light of this chapter and its topics, how might you act differently? Think differently? Feel differently? Relate differently?

sALVATION iS hEARING?

dUSTIN mETCALF

I once knew a guy who was filled with optimism that he could change the world—or at the very least, his part of the world. Some said his optimism was born out of a youthful naïveté. He was young, after all, fresh out of seminary, and in his first full-time pastoral assignment. If you knew this guy, however, you would have known that his optimism was not rooted in himself. He knew his flaws well, and he understood that he himself was not the answer. But he believed that he had committed his life to a message that *was the answer*.

"If only people could hear that God loves them," he said. "If they could hear this, change could take place. Lives could be transformed, salvation could occur . . ."

It did not take long, however, for this young man to find limits to his optimism. As he preached week after week about God's love, forgiveness, grace, and God's desire for our ongoing transformation, little change occurred. There were no dramatic, life-changing conversions.

The young pastor began to notice a disturbing fact about his congregation: there weren't very many there who had not already been saved. And here his optimism began to waiver and doubts began to creep in. "If most of the people in this church are committed Christians, why aren't we growing? Why are we not attracting others? Why is it that no one new seems to be joining our worship services and Bible studies?"

No doubt there have been many pastors who have asked these same questions. For some, their real-life circumstances knocked the optimism right out of them. Where they were once hopeful, they are now cynical. Where they were once creative, they now just go through the motions.

I've been there myself. I know what it means to pour my whole self into a cause that I deeply believe is transformative. Yet little transformation seemed to occur. I know what it means to spend hour upon hour tilling the soil of my congregation. I know what it's like to wait, hope, and pray for signs of growth. I know how it feels to look impatiently down on the tiny green sprouts of faith emerging from the soil, all the while expecting to see the emergence of giant sequoias of faith.

Despite unfulfilled expectations, I remain optimistic.

I still believe that the message to which I have committed my life offers transformation. But I have had to do some redefining. If salvation is defined entirely by having the right beliefs, we and our churches will struggle with postmodernism well into the future.

Most churches I know are like islands filled with modernist Christians while surrounded by a sea of postmodern people. Often our modernist evangelism sermons fall short, because we send modernist Christians into a mission field without these missionaries knowing how to speak and think postmodern language. Is it any wonder that many of our churches simply try to survive?

My hope remains in part because I believe that our Wesleyan perspective offers a fuller view of salvation than the view that boils salvation down to having the right beliefs. This perspective gives us a point of contact with our postmodern friends, family members, and coworkers, because it also thinks of salvation as expressed in action. We cannot earn our salvation, of course, but defining salvation exclusively by having the right beliefs results in a lifeless faith with no meaningful action.

I fear that each time we demand right belief before we accept others as moving toward salvation, more people will close the door to the transformative message of Jesus Christ. Do we continue to beat that drum until no one hears?

Hearing is an interesting process. Our tendency is to think of it as the mechanics of ear and brain. For our Hebrew brothers and sisters, this is not the case. When Jesus said in Luke 14:35, "He who has ears to hear, let him hear" (NKJV), he was drawing on a long faith history that defined hearing much differently than we do.

For centuries, Jews have recited the *Shema* as recorded in Deut. 6:4: "Hear O Israel: The LORD our God, the LORD is one" (NKJV). This prayer is at the core of the Jewish faith and would have been so for Jesus. For the Jewish people it was (and is) not enough for hearing to be a matter of the mind. It is also a matter of the heart. Hearing demands obedience. It demands action, which is why Jesus repeatedly calls for hearing that goes beyond mental assent to lifestyle and action.

I can't help but wonder what would happen if we started emphasizing this aspect of salvation. What would happen if we preached sermons that focused more on community engagement than on right beliefs? What if our calls for evangelism became invitations to become loving friends with our neighbors and co-workers? What if we started going to where sinners hang out and befriending them, instead of expecting them to come to us?

I certainly want my actions to lead to opportunities to open the door for conversations about belief. But I'm not sure that this needs to be my primary concern. I want to start by loving others. I don't think I've failed to evangelize and lead others to salvation if I fail to lead them first in "the sinner's prayer."

We all know our culture is in desperate need of Jesus. We know that our world desperately needs to hear Good News. But if they aren't likely to listen to our creeds and complex theologies, maybe it's time to emphasize preaching Christ through our hands and feet and hearts. When my salvation and your salvation are put into action, the result will be lives transformed by God. And it also creates transformed communities, a transformed country, and a transformed world.

Am I being too optimistic?

qUESTIONS

1. Should Christians be optimistic?

2. What might your neighbors and coworkers say about the optimism of the gospel as we often preach and portray it? Would you dare to ask them how "good" our Good News sounds to them?

3. How do you seek a balance between living out your beliefs and sharing verbally what those beliefs might mean?

4. How might evangelism be different if the author is right that relationships should often be established before the Christian's beliefs are presented?

5. What do you think of the idea that salvation can be more or less full?

aPPLICATION

In light of this chapter and its topics, how might you act differently? Think differently? Feel differently? Relate differently?

hOLINESS iN tHE tWENTY-fIRST cENTURY

lOST iN tRANSLATION?

bRENT pETERSON

I ask students in my Introduction to Theology course to answer this question, "Are any of you perfect?" I encourage those who consider themselves perfect to raise their hands to identify themselves.

In response, my usually fidgety students become statues. Only those wanting a laugh from the class stretch a hand upward.

So I ask you, Are you perfect?

Few readers would answer yes to my question. Yet within Holiness denominations, we find remnants of a theology of perfection. Phrases such as "Christian perfection," "holy love," and "perfect love" linger. These phrases describe a doctrine with perhaps an even more intimidating title, *entire sanctification.*

The pressing question today is not simply if these theological phrases will survive. One might wonder if God used the doctrine of entire sanctification for a season, intending that today it should be set aside.

On the contrary, I think the message of holiness and the doctrine of entire sanctification need and will be kept alive. The ideas behind these phrases declare the possibility of the world's hope and transformation.

The doctrine of entire sanctification and the holiness message can help restore us to loving God and all people as neighbors, while also helping us care for God's nonhuman world. I affirm this, because I believe that God and God's transforming and life-giving love resides at the center of holiness.

Many Holiness groups no longer talk, sing, and preach holiness—at least not consciously. I am convinced a primary reason for this is that much of the grammar, content, and imagery that once were used have proven unhelpful and even false. Such imagery, content, and grammar may have been helpful at one time and may even help a few today. But I am not optimistic it can or should be used anymore.

Here are a few phrases and ideas that seem unhelpful:

1. *Entire sanctification is guaranteed sinless perfection.* It's difficult to make this claim biblically. And John Wesley did not think that Christians ever reached a point on this earth that they no longer need to confess their sins and continually rely upon God's renewing grace.

2. *Entire sanctification is a static state of grace.* Never does a person in this lifetime "arrive," in the sense of needing no additional growth. Paul puts it well in Phil. 3:14 when he says that the Spirit empowers Christians to keep pressing toward the goal. Wesley was also clear that everyone should continually grow in Christlikeness, being renewed into the image of God.

3. *Entire sanctification is a one-size-fits-all experience.* Wesley identified different points of spiritual maturity. Yet he did not demand that everyone's journey look the same. This approach is consistent with the diversity of experience we find among the saints described in the Bible and in the Christian tradition today.

So what images and models of holiness and entire sanctification might translate the hope of the gospel effectively today? I think the Bible can help us answer this question.

The primary Old Testament word for holy is *kadosh*. This word is most often used to say that God is not a creature and to describe Israel as being set apart. The Greek term *hagios* in the

New Testament also suggests being set apart or consecrated. The Church and its people are holy when set apart doing God's will. So what is God's will?

A classic holiness text is Matt. 5:48: "Be perfect . . . as your heavenly Father is perfect" (NRSV). The word perfect is *telos*, which relates to the Old Testament word *tam* or *tamim*. Neither of these words translated as perfect means without flaw, blemish, or mistake. Instead, they mean accomplishing a goal or purpose. Something is perfect when doing what it was created to do.

My glasses are perfect, in this sense, when they are on my face and helping me see. If I used my glasses as a doorstop or soccer ball, I would profane them. And this misuse would likely destroy them.

The Bible says that we are created in God's image and thus created to love God and others. We are then perfect (doing what God created us to do) when we love. John Wesley described Christian perfection by affirming that our tempers (attitudes and actions) would be restored so that eventually our first responses in the moments we live our lives would not be selfish, but the first or "normal" response would be to love God and neighbor. This is what it means to grow into Christlikeness—it is the hope of holiness.

As a person grows in grace, he or she almost inevitably comes to a moment or series of moments when he or she is offered the chance to become entirely devoted to God in love. Nothing should be held back. Wesley encourages Christians to consecrate their lives fully to God. The idea is not so much that we get more of God, but God gets more—in fact all—of us.

If the sanctified person chooses sin rather than love, that choice is abnormal. Lovelessness becomes an aberration, a mistake. Saints who sin must quickly confess and repent and seek greater levels of maturity.

The hope of entire sanctification is profoundly beautiful, centered on loving God and others. But like all theological doctrines, it should be viewed more like a piece of art or poetry. It is not a process of mechanization or an automation system of spiritual formation. While everyone needs to be renewed and restored into the image of God, each person's journey is unique.

The good news of the gospel proclaims forgiveness for all forms of sinfulness, which all involve failing to love God, others, and ourselves. But it also proclaims freedom from the power of sin and death.

My hope is that these models and images of holiness will prevent the doctrine from becoming lost in translation in a postmodern age. And they become tools in the process of our becoming perfected in love as we love God and neighbors as ourselves.

qUESTIONS

1. How do you handle the Bible's command that we be perfect? What do you think it means?

2. What language and ideas about holiness or sanctification have been helpful to you? What has been unhelpful?

3. What do you think of the Wesleyan emphasis upon becoming free in this life from the power of sin?

4. Do you think the idea that love is at the heart of holiness is helpful or unhelpful? Does it provide clarity or only muddy the water?

aPPLICATION

In light of this chapter and its topics, how might you act differently? Think differently? Feel differently? Relate differently?

iNDIVIDUALS aND cOMMUNITIES

cHRISTA kLOSTERMAN

Most of us would not have to look very far to find people searching for significant relationships in life. We could name a friend, a coworker, or a neighbor who is looking for meaning by connecting with others. These folks are tired of feeling lonely and dealing with past broken relationships. They want to feel that they belong; they want to be part of a family. They want friends who will be there through the good times and bad.

Many in our increasingly postmodern culture possess a deep hunger to be a part of a community. We all want to belong.

When I see that hunger for connection in the eyes of those around me, I become convinced that the Church has something valuable to offer. The Church can respond to this need, not as a sales pitch to register people on the membership roles, but as a deep answer to loneliness and brokenness. Community is at the heart of the Church's identity. When I see the relational hunger around us, I start to see that the Church can have a bright future.

Love, after all, is at the center of Jesus' message. Love God. Love one another. Love our enemies. Love ourselves.

A faith whose chief command is love has much to say about relationships. From the beginning, the Church was instructed to care for each other. Christians are called to live side by side, to work as a team in sharing God's transforming love.

This is what Jesus did in his ministry. He collected a group of people and made them disciples. They ate together, traveled together, learned together, and ministered to those around them. Jesus passed this way of *being* on to his disciples, and he told them to continue with the help of the Holy Spirit. His intention was that, in his absence, we might live together as the Body of Christ on earth. And living in this way includes inviting others into our life together.

Somewhere along the way the Church has neglected togetherness as part of our identity. We still commit ourselves to attending worship, studying the Bible, and doing ministry. But it has become easy to discount the value of relationships with those who come with us. We have far too easily thought we could be *doing* Christianity all alone.

Many of us have been so busy trying to get "the important things" done that we haven't seen all the value that exists just in coming together. We study, worship, and minister without recognizing the importance found in sharing life together.

Church can sometimes seem like a venture in filling our heads with data helpful only if by chance we were chosen to appear on the *Jeopardy* game show. We have emphasized the acquisition of "knowledge" as the most important need. But often our greatest need is to be connected with fellow disciples. We need to challenge, comfort, struggle, and share burdens with each other. We have attempted to do ministry *to* others without realizing that ministry is something that can flow *between* us in relationship.

Thankfully, we have not always ignored the communal side of our Christian faith. There are many contemporary congregations who emphasize community, especially those in rural areas. But chances are we can all do a better job of sharing life together.

We have models both from the distant past and in the present that can help. These models suggest that we start building community by being more aware of each other when we gather for worship or ministry, or even as we do projects. Just tending to relationships as we come together are small shifts that can have a large effect.

Telling our stories, praying for one another, eating together, and designating specific times for fellowship can take what we already do and help develop a greater sense of community. We may not need to "add" anything to what we already do. Perhaps we need to tend more closely to our usual practices, believing that this attention will take us deeper into one another's lives. And this attention to practices may become crucial to our efforts to welcome others into our Christian family.

Intentional attempts to build community will produce fruit. But life in the midst of community is not always easy. Perhaps one reason we have not worked on building the relationships is that we know that relationships can sometimes be difficult. After all, we do not always see eye to eye. We offend each other. We fail each other. It is rather easy to hurt one another.

But here I think Christian community can shine brightest among any alternatives. Although each of us has sharp edges, the Christian narrative that brings us together gives insight into how we ought to deal with each other. Living life in love together is so central to our faith that much of what Jesus teaches us orients around how we must live to keep relationships intact.

Jesus calls us to be humble and gentle, patient and kind. Following Jesus means that we will offer mercy and compassion. We make confession and offer forgiveness. Although relationships can be hard work, living in a Christian community that practices these virtues offers us more sense of belonging than any alternative.

Practicing the ways of living together taught in Scripture will help us build a stronger and wider community. As the Church moves into an increasingly postmodern world, we have reason for hope. If we faithfully live out our calling, those in our community-hungry culture might start seeing in us what they desperately desire for their own lives. Let's walk together.

qUESTIONS

1. Why are relationships so important?

2. Is it bad to try to be a solo Christian? Yes or no? Why?

3. What do you think of the idea that people are so desperate to belong that they will seek a group to which they can belong before they adopt any specific doctrines? What are the advantages and challenges for the church that people look to belong first and believe later?

4. How and why are relationships in the Church so difficult? Why is it necessary for the Church to be a place of love for one another?

aPPLICATION

In light of this chapter and its topics, how might you act differently? Think differently? Feel differently? Relate differently?

eVANGELISM iN tHE pOSTMODERN mATRIX

dANA hICKS

"Suppose you were to die today and stand before God, and he were to say to you, 'Why should I let you into my heaven?' What would you say?"

Over the years, I have used this question countless times in my spiritual conversations. You may recognize it as a crucial part in one of the most popular evangelistic tools of the twentieth century. It's a diagnostic question used to determine whether a person knows the right answer to an ultimate question in life.

Like many who came of age in the 1980s, I was nurtured in a faith community in which canned sales pitches and thinly veiled manipulative invitations were used to get people to say a magic prayer. That prayer was believed to keep people from going to hell when they died.

Like many others, I memorized that pitch. I confronted people I barely knew. And I swallowed hard to bury that deep-seated intuition that this whole process felt off-kilter. Deep down, I felt I was saying something that was pretty much like, "What will it take to get you into this car today?"

The truth is, I care a lot about people. I really believe that life is infinitely better when I follow Jesus. I believe that evangelism is not just something I do to get another notch in my award belt. And yet in my evangelistic journey, the good news of Jesus became associated with a lot of anxiety.

In recent years, conversation—more than confrontation—has become the evangelistic trend among emerging church leaders. For many, evangelism is becoming more respectful, more empowering, and less manipulative. This is a good thing. But this trend is not without its unintended negative consequences.

Brian McLaren's book *A New Kind of Christian* has a dialogue between Dan and Neo. And that dialogue includes this insight: "One of my mottos in life is that people are often against something worth being against, but in the process they find themselves for some things that aren't worth being for."[1]

So here is the dirty little secret about the emerging church: it's often not very good at evangelism. For all its talk about being missional, the emerging church is generally a monolithic group of burned-out, white, middle-class, college-educated, young adults who are sick of the American expression of church. Somehow being against manipulative and inauthentic evangelism has meant being the kind of person who is insular and conspicuously silent about matters of faith.

When I was a rookie pastor, I became good friends with a man named James who oversaw the local chapter of Narcotics Anonymous. As a former drug addict, James had deep compassion for those suffering from addictions of all kinds. That is why I called him when a guy named Larry visited our church.

"James, I have this guy who came to church. I think he might be a drug user. Can you meet with the two of us and give me some insight?" James quickly agreed and we set up a time for coffee at the local Duffy's restaurant.

After brief introductions in a window booth, James awkwardly stirred his coffee and said, "So, Larry, when are you going to stop using?" Both Larry and I were stunned at James's frankness.

"I'm not using," said Larry. He smiled and shifted uncomfortably on the cheap vinyl bench.

"When are you going to stop lying to yourself and others?" James said, without batting an eye.

Just as I was beginning to regret bringing James to this meeting, Larry dropped his head and began to confess his addictions. It was one of those rare moments of both truth and grace. James became a conduit of God's grace to a broken man in desperate need of reality.

As we stood later in the parking lot, I said to James, "What was that all about?" To which James gave me words that have formed my way of understanding church ever since, ("We don't do people favors by ignoring their self-destructive behavior.")

Drug addiction may be an extreme example. But I believe that if we are serious about loving the people God has placed in our paths, it may mean more than just accepting them. It will likely mean having difficult conversations with people about their self-destructive patterns. Not conversations from a position of superiority but conversations in a spirit of love and compassion.

I think sharing the Good News means both accepting and affirming people as human beings. But it also means helping them escape their own self-destructive sin. Jesus' words in John 8:11 to the woman caught in adultery illustrate this difficult balance: "Neither do I condemn you," to which he adds, "go and sin no more" (NKJV).

So how does one reframe evangelism in the postmodern era to reflect our loving hopes for our world? How do we both speak the truth and do it in love?

Simple formulas probably cannot encapsulate the line we must walk. But a good place to begin may be to rethink the questions we ask in our spiritual conversations. Perhaps we should add these to our list of diagnostic evangelism questions:

1. **"If you knew you were going to live another forty years, what kind of person would you want to become?"**
This question reimagines the infamous evangelism question about why any of us should get into heaven when we die. Maybe because we live in a society that sterilizes death and removes us from the experience of dying, many people do not agonize over death.

Focusing evangelism on what happens to us after we die tends to create disciples who are not concerned with either whom they are becoming or the kind of world they will leave behind. Of course, we may die tonight. But it is much more likely that we will live a while longer—a decade or two or three or more. What happens in the meantime? Will we live an abundant life? What kind of legacy will we leave behind?

2. **"If you could know what God is doing in the world, would you want to be part of it?"**

I have been asking this question a lot lately. And I've never had anyone answer by saying, "No!"

I like this question, because it focuses evangelism on God's agenda instead of our tendency to get God to care about our agendas. I also like this question because it opens the door to talk about what Jesus talked about the most—the kingdom of God breaking in to our world right now.

The modernist style of evangelism focused on right answers. That is, Christians wanted to hear the right answer from others about who Jesus is. Or they wanted the right answer to questions about what it takes to get a ticket to heaven.

People seem to be asking different questions these days. The questions focus less on "Is it true?" and more about "Does it work?" Paul's posture in 1 Cor. 12:31 to a pluralistic, premodern world can probably help us engage our own postmodern world. Before a description of what the way of love looks like, Paul said "Let me *show* you a more excellent way . . ." (emphasis added).

qUESTIONS

1. Do you agree with the author that the dirty little secret of the postmodern church is its lack of evangelism? Explain your answer.

✳ 2. What qualities made James's straightforward question to Larry appropriate in an awkward moment between strangers? What can we learn from James?

3. How receptive might your unchurched family, neighbors, and coworkers be to the author's two main questions? Would you dare ask them at an appropriate time?

4. What do you think the author means when he says that the kingdom of God is breaking into our world right now?

aPPLICATION

In light of this chapter and its topics, how might you act differently? Think differently? Feel differently? Relate differently?

cHRISTIANITY aND oTHER rELIGIONS

aLBERT tRUESDALE

For many evangelicals, Oprah Winfrey posed a surprising question in the title of her 2008 online course "Are You Ready to Be Awakened?"

Kelley, a Roman Catholic, had been reading Eckhart Tolle's book *The New Earth*. Energized by the book's spiritual riches, Kelley believed it offered paths to spiritual growth inaccessible through Christianity. She eagerly asked the famous talk show host, "How do you reconcile these spiritual teachings with Christian beliefs?"

Oprah answered that long ago she removed God from a Christian "box." Knowing God, she said, requires exploring many spiritual paths.

If Christians limit their "spirituality" to Christianity, Oprah insists, they will misunderstand Jesus. Jesus did not intend for people to treat him as God. He "came to give us some principles or laws for living," Oprah said. "He showed us Christ-consciousness, the way of the heart and the higher consciousness."[1]

Oprah is a fine representative of religious pluralism, a prominent feature of our postmodern age. Religious pluralism has at least three meanings.

First, it describes recognition of the religious diversity evident in our social "backyards." We come face-to-face with many religions and religious people.

Second, religious pluralism describes how the multiplicity of religions has become a fixture in our social consciousness. Religious diversity is just "the way life is."

Finally, it names for many people the way things "ought to be." There "ought" to be many religious options, because no single religion can embody the rich universe of religious insights. All religions contain important truths, so this thinking goes, and devotees of one religion "ought" to respect another.

Religious pluralism forces Christians to ask, "What is the relationship between Christianity and other world religions?" Some Christians embrace religious pluralism as the way things "ought to be." For instance, George Regas says that "not only is the exclusive claim that Christ is the only way to God and saving faith a distortion of the total biblical message, it is the source of the most deadly conflicts over the centuries. . . . I can no longer think about Jesus as the only way to God and to a saving faith."[2] But other Christians believe they must hold fast to what Regas rejects.

 How should we in the Wesleyan theological tradition answer the question regarding the relationship between Christianity and other religions? Wesleyans affirm the primacy of biblical authority for faith and practice. Perhaps the most important question related to religious pluralism is, "Who does the Bible affirm Jesus Christ to be?" The primary question has not to do with Christianity as a religion but with Christ as a person.)

In John 20:28, the disciple Thomas confesses that Jesus is both "Lord" and "God." His enemies fiercely disagree, noting that Jesus makes himself equal to God (5:18-19) and makes himself God (10:33-34). Why does the Fourth Gospel affirm Jesus' equality with God? It does so because Jesus repeatedly demonstrates the possession of God's creative and judgmental power.

In John 5:1-16, Jesus performs a miracle on the Sabbath. He is accused of calling God his own Father, which seems to make himself equal with God. Jesus denies that he is acting independently of God. On his own, the Son can do nothing (v. 19).

Jesus does what he sees the Father doing (vv. 19-20). Whatever powers Jesus possesses have come directly from his Father. He enjoys the same honor as God, the same authority, and the same extraordinary powers. He makes alive (v. 21), has had all judgment assigned to him (v. 22), honors the Father (v. 23), raises the dead (v. 25), has life in himself (v. 26), and executes judgment (v. 27). Raising the dead, judging, and having life in oneself (vv. 28-29) refer to the power God would exercise to conclude salvation history.

In recounting Abraham's great faith in Rom. 4:17, the apostle Paul includes two affirmations: God exercised creative power by calling into existence, and God exercised power by raising the dead. John's Gospel attributes those same powers to Christ. Jesus can now be called Lord, the divine name associated with that power. The full force of the confession is to acclaim Christ as the Creator God who alone has life in himself. This cannot be said of any other god or any other redeemer.

Like Thomas, we in the Wesleyan tradition affirm uncompromisingly that Christ is both "Lord and God." We do this in response to God's own definitive self-disclosure, not because Christianity creates the affirmation. God acted to reconcile the world to God's own self. Jesus alone is the wisdom and power of God. In Jesus alone is there salvation. We well know that this affirmation is as offensive and scandalous today as it was in the first century.

For Wesleyans, our confession of faith in Christ is also Trinitarian. We believe that unceasingly and universally the Holy Spirit works in both individuals and through institutions. The Spirit bears invitational witness to the crucified, risen, ascended, and coming Christ. This is God's evangelical work, occurring even before we can detect it.

Wesleyans clearly recognize the importance of evangelical conversion resulting from a Spirit-inspired proclamation of the gospel. But we set no limits on how or when the Spirit will accomplish God's purposes. In various ways and measures, the Spirit can preveniently (i.e., with anticipation) employ religions—and any other device God chooses—in service to the gospel. Many remarkable stories of Christ's work prior to the gospel's explicit proclamation convince us to place no limits upon the Spirit's creative witness to Christ.

Wesleyans do not "baptize" or authenticate other religions as independent paths to God. But we do believe that some religions seem to be more amenable to the Spirit's anticipatory work than others. For instance, Pure Land Buddhism teaches that Amitabba Buddha is pure love and that he offers salvation by divine grace through faith. By grace Amitabba sets believers free from vainly seeking for peace through strenuous works. While affirming these similarities, Wesleyans do not naively ignore the darkness that continues in the absence of Christ revealed in his fullness.

In summary, a Wesleyan answer regarding Christianity and other religions contains four elements.

First, we affirm the New Testament's witness to Jesus Christ as God incarnate.

Second, we affirm that the promised Spirit of God unfailingly and creatively acts in the world. The Spirit seeks to draw all people to eternal life in Christ and prepares the way for the gospel's proclamation. We must seek to discern and cultivate the Spirit's work.

Third, we affirm that religions can become vehicles the Holy Spirit uses to draw people to Christ. But religions are at best incomplete anticipations of the fullness of God manifest in Christ.

Finally, we Wesleyans abhor mean-spirited opposition to other religions. Instead, we seek to understand and dialogue with those from other religions. We dialogue because we want to serve, not obstruct, the Redeemer's prevenient work.

qUESTIONS

1. Map the ten religious groups located closest to your local church. Historically, how has your congregation chosen to interact with these other denominations and/or religions?

2. Why are so many Christians reluctant to build relationships with those of other religions?

3. What are the upsides and downsides to the quest of those, like Oprah, who seek various ways to be awakened spiritually?

4. How might God use another religion to draw people to Christ? How important is our role in helping others find the love of God revealed in the fullness of Jesus Christ?

aPPLICATION

In light of this chapter and its topics, how might you act differently? Think differently? Feel differently? Relate differently?

Great questions to consider for paper!

cRITICAL rESPONSE— tIMELESS tRUTHS iN cONTEMPORARY fORMS

gENE gRATE

It is no surprise to hear searching questions about God and the Bible from the postmodern generation. Influenced by a world that largely does not accept truth as absolute and believes that Jesus may not be the only way to God, they become skeptical of religious pat answers. Such skepticism forces one to step back and evaluate the accepted expressions and explanations of truth. The goal in responding to their concerns is not to set aside truth as we know it but to reinvent ways to communicate it.

When considering the Bible's trustworthy authority, what can be confusing are the seemingly broad interpretations of biblical passages shaped by the historical perspectives of time, culture, and context (such as Lyons-Pardue's reference to the American slavery debate). It is not that truth changes with circumstances; rather, those who view it do so through the lens of personal experience. Even so, the essence of the truth remains unaltered.

Human relationships open a window of light for understanding our relationship with God, who is the source of all truth. Andrew Pottenger, my son-in-law and Nazarene Theological Seminary student, helped bring clarity to this issue. He noted that when getting to know someone, we may only know a name or have limited knowledge of the person. Based on such limited knowledge and experience, certain assumptions are made that may or may not be accurate. However, the truth about the person doesn't change. He or she is who he or she is regardless of our assumptions or perspectives. The more we learn, the more our assumptions are either confirmed or modified. Likewise, the truth about God doesn't change; we simply learn more about him, either as he reveals more or as we simply grow in our understanding. Our assumptions about God may change, but God himself does not. He is the same yesterday, today, and forever.

In a similar way, the broad interpretations of biblical passages shaped by historical perspectives of time, culture, and context must not mislead one to believe that truth is relative or can be altered. Rather, it becomes an inspiring reminder that there are many different ways to perceive, express, and apply biblical truth. Sometimes this is due to God's progressive revelation of himself and his will for us; at others times it reflects our maturing faith. Kara Lyons-Pardue makes a strong point by saying the most vital context as readers of Scripture is the Church, the community of faith. As we read, pray, debate, and sing these biblical passages in the context of a believing community, the ministering presence of the Holy Spirit enlightens believers with meaning and truth that is contemporary for that generation.

The active presence of the Holy Spirit in the world is what makes the Bible such a dynamic book, worthy of our complete trust. It is a living document, "breathed" upon by God himself. The apostle Paul wrote to his protégé, Timothy, "All Scripture is inspired by God and is useful to teach us what is true" (2 Tim. 3:16, NLT). Jesus also said, "And I will ask the Father, and he will give you another Advocate, who will never leave you. He is the Holy Spirit, who leads into all truth" (John 14:16-17, NLT).

When answering the postmodern question about biblical authority, the greatest testament to its trustworthiness is each person who has staked his or her life on its teaching and truth. Their daily faith in God that has transformed their lives puts to rest many arguments and debates.

Since our Wesleyan faith perspective motivates us to share our faith with pre-Christians, we often are baffled at the many who lack the desire to do so and the meager results when they do. If it is God's will that no one should die in his or her sins, but receive eternal life in Christ (John 3:16), then we must ask why more don't come to Christ when someone tells them of God's love.

Dustin Metcalf frames this concern with the need to engage postmodernists with the gospel of Christ in words and actions they understand. It is simplistic at best and misleading at worst to believe that a one-size gospel presentation fits all. It is naive to think that words alone can convince a person to leave a life of sin (which may not be recognized as sin) and run into the arms of Jesus. Although right beliefs are important when telling others about Christ, the postmodern person looks for attitudes and actions that support the words. To such a person, attitudes and actions born from God's love are far more convincing than religious arguments or presentations. Even Wesley emphasized the need for both a personal holiness based on right beliefs and a social holiness expressed in loving attitudes and actions. Authentic Christian faith is a bridge to the heart of God and to the spiritual needs of the world.

To make the issue of evangelism even more complex, many believers confuse biblical word pictures, and this leads to unintended results. For example, one could say that holiness is a call to heart purity and to be "set apart" for acts of spiritual service. However, this imagery is often confused to mean "come apart," thus encouraging the isolation of the church from the world. Such confusion can cause the church to see itself as a fortress, a refuge from the dangers of a sinful world. A fortress is a shelter and protection for those within, a haven to preserve the preferences and way of life for its citizens. Outsiders are viewed with suspicion, a potential threat to the status quo. They may be welcomed but often reluctantly. With this perspective, a church may become ingrown, having little or no concern for those outside its walls. This could explain, to some degree, the lack of desire to share God's love with those who do not yet know God.

Martin Luther, the great Reformer, wrote the beloved hymn, "A Mighty Fortress Is Our God." Its message focuses our theology. Throughout the Bible, the *fortress* for believers has been God himself, not the church. David expressed this belief well, "The LORD is my rock, my fortress, and my savior; my God is my rock, in whom I find protection" (2 Sam. 22:2-3, NLT).

By contrast, the church most accurately reflects its holiness to the postmodern world when it becomes a spiritual hospital for the world's sin-sick. Its primary concern is to receive the sin-sick and nurture them to spiritual health in Christ. Even Jesus said, "Healthy people don't need a doctor—sick people do. I have come to call not those who think they are righteous, but those who know they are sinners" (Mark 2:17, NLT). As a spiritual hospital, our acts of love and compassion speak louder than our evangelistic words to the postmodern person. As Dustin Metcalf rightly observes, this kind of evangelism is preaching Christ with our hands, feet, and hearts.

Our evangelistic responsibility, however, does not end with people making decisions for Christ but continues as the church seeks to make disciples from those decisions. In this book, Christa Klosterman addresses the need for community in helping people with both the decisions and the growth. In response to this increasing awareness, many churches are developing methods to enhance Christian community. More traditionally, churches have offered Sunday School at a set time weekly and encouraged members to learn more about the Bible, with a light touch on relationships. Again, one size is unlikely to fit all needs.

Many churches now additionally offer a small-group ministry that encourages members to meet at those times throughout the week that work best with individual schedules. Longtime members or postmodern converts are invited into a small-group experience where God's Word is explored and there is a greater emphasis on community. They share real-life experiences, pray for each other, eat together, and share fellowship in creative ways. This model not only meets the need to *know* God's Word but also helps each person *be a doer* of the Word. Other churches are blending these two models, where Sunday School classes allocate half of their class time to the lesson and the other half to discussion of the lesson and prayer in small groups.

The Early Church also faced these issues. Acts 2:42 reminds us, "They devoted themselves to the apostles' teaching and to the fellowship, to the breaking of bread and to prayer" (NIV). It was their way of addressing issues of doctrine along with the personal and community needs of each disciple.

To further speak to this issue for the contemporary postmodern mind, Dana Hicks reminds us there is a greater interest in a faith that works than a system of right beliefs. Indeed, both are important and one should not contradict the other. True faith in God does work in the human heart and life. As Hicks points out, after the apostle Paul shared his beliefs with the difficult Corinthian church, he confidently said, "And now I will show you the most excellent way" (1 Cor. 12:31, NIV). Paul reinforced his words with actions. Indeed, Christian community provides the right context to bring beliefs and actions together.

Another issue the contemporary Wesleyan church wrestles with is the ability to express and explain the holiness message and doctrine of entire sanctification. Interestingly, this challenge is not new. John Wesley had to find a way to the hearts of his generation with this life-changing truth. One should not conclude that the doctrine is no longer relevant because some people seem confused by models and images that worked a generation ago but do not bring clarity to the postmodern mind. Brent Peterson tells us why this issue is so important when he wrote in this book, "The ideas behind these phrases declare the possibility of the world's hope and transformation." Even Jesus communicated the Old Testament law in contemporary models and images that convinced people of their spiritual needs, inspiring them to turn to God. We must remember that the message is timeless, but methods and models should be contemporary and meaningful for every generation. It is a matter with eternal consequences.

As Wesleyans, we must not fail to understand the mind-set of our secular culture. Albert Truesdale points out that, for many, believing in Christ is only one of many ways leading to God. This religious pluralism competes with our testimony that "the free gift of God is eternal life through Christ Jesus our Lord" (Rom.6:23, NLT). It discredits Jesus' own claim, "No one can come to the Father except through me" (John 14:6, NLT). Such skepticism about Christ can open doors to many conversations about Jesus. Our Wesleyan faith provides both the framework and motivation to enter into such conversations, bringing hope and help for those seeking God.

(Truth has no expiration date. Something that was true 2,000 years ago is still true today. If it was true, it is still true, and it will always be true.)Neither time, nor cultures, nor contexts can alter truth. People can relate to it, reflect upon it, wrestle with it, interpret it, make assumptions about it—but they cannot alter it. John Wesley is claimed to have said, "If it's true, it's not new. If it's new, it's not true."

(Whether a person has lived in the premodern, modern, or postmodern culture, the challenge has been the same—to communicate timeless truths in contemporary forms that allow God to educate the mind and transform the heart. We must be biblically accurate and culturally relevant. Interestingly, Jesus was both.)

qUESTION

What do you find helpful or unhelpful in this critical response?

cONVERSATION iGNITER
mri mIRACLES cONTINUED

lEONARD sWEET

In the midst of a world gripped by the Calvinist belief in predestination came the Wesleyan notion of human perfectibility, which was essentially a theology of change. We can change our future. We can change our destiny. We can change our interiors. We can whip up the world to suit divine truth (or, more perversely, our own tastes). The Methodist Revolution reintroduced a theology of change into the bloodstream of Christianity.

What is a "theology of change"? Let me approach it from another angle.

How old are you?

Your best answer is: "About 15.5 years."

That's the average age of your body. Very little (if any) of your body has been around since you were born. Your body is constantly changing. Your body is not the same as it was a year ago. Your body is not the same as it was yesterday. Your cheek cells (mucus membranes) are flushed down your gullet three times a day. Your epithelial cells lining the gut are replaced every five days; your epidermal skin cells covering the surface of your body are replaced every two weeks; your red blood cells every 120 days.[1] Your entire skeleton is replaced every 10 years. The real question is, How many bodies do you go through in a lifetime?

By the time you die, there is nothing left of the "original" you . . . but you. The paradox of life is this: in order for you to stay the same you have to change.

The best definition of a "living thing" is "something that can die."[2] Humans live by dying. The defining characteristic of the dead is that they do not change. The defining characteristic of someone who is "alive" is constant change. You are not the same person you were a year ago, or a day ago . . . . or even a minute ago. The more alive you are, the more change you undergo. The more you embrace life, the more you embrace change.[3]

The paradox of the gospel is this: it is always the same, and always changing. You might even say that an alive church dies more than a dead church. If the "alternative to a changed society is darkness," as some historians have argued,[4] the alternative to a changed church is death. The church needs death therapy if it is to thrive in a Google world.

✽ ✽ ✽

It seems that all true things must change and
that only that which changes remains true.
Carl Jung[5]

✽ ✽ ✽

Learning is a process of change. Change is continuous and discontinuous at the same time. Stage change is continuous change. State change is discontinuous change. Some parts of our being are going through stage change; others through state change. But if we are "learners" we are constantly changing.

"Growth" and "transformation" are fancy names for "change." The primary meaning of "disciple" (*mathetes*) is "learner." Jesus said, "Learn from me." Nobody ought to understand or embrace change better than Christians, because that is at the heart of what it means to "follow me." In fact, "conversion" is a theological word for "change." The gospel is all about humans being "changed and rearranged" by the power of salvation. Poets like Gerard Manley Hopkins may speak of how "the world is charged with the grandeur of God," but Christians speak of how the world is both charged and changed by the grandeur (and grace) of God.

Evangelists are best defined as change agents for God. If there ever were change experts, it ought to be disciples of Jesus. Changed lives are the speciality of Jesus followers. The church is in the change business.

If you have ever seen the Canadian "Red Green Show," you have heard the "Man's Prayer."

I'm a man
I can change
If I have to
I guess . . .

For a Gutenberg church to move into a Google world, it must learn another version of the "Man's Prayer." I call it the "Church Prayer":

I'm a church
I can change
If I have to
I guess . . .

✽ ✽ ✽

**If our ideas are mainly small, weak, superficial and incoherent, life will appear insipid, uninteresting, petty and chaotic.[6]
Economist E. F. Schumacher**

✽ ✽ ✽

Who would disagree that the church needs new strategies and structures to meet new challenges as change races and rages across the face of the planet? For some, this Google world is a time when everything seems to be unbolted. For others, this Google world is a time when everything seems to be in bud. For the first, there is a fear of falling and coming loose, and the attendant quixotic quests for restoring the "original" state of affairs. For the second, there are openings to the future that are grabbed like a trapeze swinging from the future to save you from a fall.

In the past two decades, "change studies" have become so sophisticated in their methodologies that they have achieved almost scientific status. Based on research done by John Kotter of Harvard, Dean Ornish of UC-San Francisco, and George Lakoff of UC-Berkeley, scholars have concluded that there are three key ingredients for lasting, transformative change: the MAGNETISM of a Big Dream, the RESONANCE of emotional engagement, the use of IMAGING to reframe the present to fit it for the future.[7]

If your church is to navigate this transition from a Gutenberg to a Google world with integrity and lasting transformation, you will need an MRI Miracle: the raw inspiration of Magnetic dreams, the intense commitment and emotional engagement that comes from Resonant hope, and the creativity that comes from reframing Images.

MRI miracles are simple, but not easy. Simple is not easy to accomplish or apply. While the gospel is by nature Magnetic, Resonant, and Imaging, it is not easy to get the church to go in for an MRI treatment.

mAGNETIC

What gets you up to greet the midnight hour? What keeps you awake to burn the midnight oil? What gets you to take a breathtaking gamble on the future?

Man-On-The-Moon dreams. Not half-measures, or puny, pint-sized goals. But amphetamine ambitions, great expectations, heroic imaginations of operatic sweep, swing-for-the-fence endeavors. The only way change happens is when humans imagine a different world, when they dream soul-sized dreams that nurture the human spirit. The primary challenge of the church in a Google world is to live a magnetic faith in a demagnetized world.

Contrary to almost everything we've been taught about how to get people to change, "radical, sweeping, comprehensive changes are often easier for people than small, incremental ones," says Alan Deutschman in *Fast Company*.[8] The discovery of the "M" in the "MRI" comes to the world of change studies from the medical community. Dean Ornish has researched why two-thirds of patients prescribed one of the wonder-working statin drugs stop taking them within one year. The reason is that statins "Roto-Rooter" the veins silently and without visible changes. Small changes in life (popping a pill)—especially changes that don't show visible effects—are harder to sustain than big changes that require lifestyle alterations.[9]

This need for big dreams does not minimize the importance of small steps and small-scale victories. In fact, other research has shown that the bigger the dream, the bigger the need for "short-term wins" (John Kotter), which keep people feeling the radical nature of the changes taking place and open them to risk.[10] But small steps won't move us very far in the right direction if the system hasn't changed and been reframed. Small steps will not be taken without the encompassing "big picture" and extreme dream.

✳ ✳ ✳

"Guess the world needs its dreamers, may they never wake up."
'80s English pop band Prefab Sprout, "Cars & Girls"

✳ ✳ ✳

Take the awakening of the world and the church to creation care. To buy a Prius, or put up some solar panels, or recycle better are things that move us toward deeper shades of green. But unless there is a Green Dream in which we eliminate the very concept of "waste" itself and realize that nothing is "waste," that there is no "away" to which to throw things, and that Jesus himself opposed the category of "waste" ("Gather up the fragments left over, that nothing may be lost" [John 6:12, NRSV]), we may be full of "sound and fury" but "signify nothing." In the words of the Canadian ecologist William Rees (who coined the term "ecological footprint" in 1992), "We're all on the same ship, and what we do in our individual cabins is of almost no consequences in terms of the direction the ship is going."[11]

For change to take place there needs to be the magnetism of a big dream that will change our direction. I call it a da Vincian dream with a Michelangelo-ian passion.

Where did Michelangelo get the energy to paint a 40-meter ceiling virtually single-handed for four years? He wrote home in July 1512, three months before the ceiling's completion, "I work harder than any man who ever lived." Michelangelo had an acute sense of life's brevity. To one apprentice, he signed a sketch with these words: "Draw, Antonio, draw, Antonio, draw and don't waste time."

Daniel Burnham was the architect whose planning was primarily responsible for the rebuilding of Chicago after the Great Fire. These are Burnham's thoughts, present in the aftermath of the Chicago Fire of 1871, not present enough in the aftermath of our cultural tsunamis and hurricanes and floods: "Make no little plans; they have no magic to stir men's blood. . . . Make big plans: aim high in hope and work."[12]

People need the next BIG THING, the next BIG IDEA, the next BIG DREAM.[13]

We are deeply ambivalent about ambition. One moment, we criticize a kid with the words "he's got no ambition;" the next moment we criticize another kid with these words, "he's ambitious, you know." Or we use that powerful metaphor, "vaulting ambition" by which we mean a "vaulting ambition that o'erleaps itself." In fact, at one point Paul warns a rebellious church to "make it your ambition to have no ambition."[14]

But rightly understood it's not our ambitiousness that is going to ruin us. It's our lack of ambition. Life gets quickly miniaturized, and the "smallness" that was in Zacchaeus—"a small man"[15] refers to more than just his height—starts miniaturizing and mediocritizing us. To the smallness in each of us—small of spirit, small of dreams, small of hope—the gospel shouts, "Come down and Grow up! Reach Full Stature!" At what point do our ambitions stretch no further than Hummer houses in the suburbs? At what point do Christians settle for ordinary, run-of-the-mill lives? At what point do preachers settle for ordinary, run-of-the-mill ministries? At what point do "converts" become lumpen laity that settle for ordinary, run-of-the-mill churches?

Whatever you can do or dream you can, begin it. Boldness has genius, power and magic in it. Begin it now!
Attributed to German playwright/philosopher
Johann Wolfgang von Goethe[16]

✣ ✣ ✣

Absence of ambition spawns a life of anxiety. That word "anxiety" comes from the Latin word *angustia* which means narrowness. It's the narrowness of our expectations, our confining God to narrow categories and hamstringing of the Holy Spirit, which issues in anxiety. When anxiety rules the church, the church will never pass up an opportunity to pass up an opportunity.[17] Hope and Shalom swell along the riverbanks where maximum dreams flow.

Bursting our narrow banks and letting the river flow is an exercise in what Alan Kreider calls "bunking."[18] It is easy for us to do "debunking," or the critique of other churches, out-of-date hair, odd notions, off-key singing. But the major task of the church is to "bunk"—to climb out on a limb and offer this Google world The Big Bunk, The Big Picture, to make connections between the past and future that combine to form a present framework for understanding and analysis. The Big Bunk is an intoxicating brew of past and present and future that is as arousing as Ammonite wine.

What is your greatest desire and dream? Is it for the advancement of your own personal kingdom? Or is it for the kingdom of God? If we are ambitious for God's glory, the church will embody a rich aspirational life. Googleys will gravitate to aspirational places and communities who paint on a big canvas pictures of a better future, clear in general no matter how cloudy in detail.

If the church is to be part of God's mission in the world, it must become a Big Picture artist. This defense of big, magnetic, mesmeric dreams is not a defense of the mega church. Just like big pictures look best in small rooms,[19] so big dreams often hang best in small spaces. But all places where the "Amen" or "So Be It!" comes to mean "Make It So!" have a role in the filling in of the Big Picture.

 "M" research that shows the power of a galvanizing dream really should not surprise Christians. The very definition of *metanoia* (repentance) is an about-face, a radical turning and re-turning of one's life toward God. Metanoia is more than an inward turning; it's a paradigm shift, a turning to get "on the way," toward the truth, in the life. If your church is not "on the way" it's "in the way" of truth and life.

Daydreams are as important to our everyday living and self-understanding as night dreams. We create our existence by our daydreams because our imagination is shaped by the images and narratives of our daydreams.

But we need to get the right dream. Every "leap forward" isn't a leap forward. "The Great Leap Forward" in China (1958-1960) caused the greatest famine in the history of the world. The dream is bigger than the "survival" of a church. Why was your church created in the first place? A dream of "balancing the budget" isn't doing "great things for God." Even a multiracial church is not a big enough I-can-do-all-things dream; why not the bigger leap forward of bettering your community?

✳ ✳ ✳

We are standing on whales, fishing for minnows.
Old Polynesian expression

✳ ✳ ✳

Jesus creates good desires, true dreams, beautiful hopes amid the prevailing cynicism and despair. "That which is seen is not hope. Why do you then hope it?" In teaching us that reality can be the daughter of dreams, and by laying out God's dream for a new heaven and a new earth—a vision of the kingdom of God—Jesus made us eschatologically motivated. Because I expect confirmation of the Bible's truth-claims in the future, I don't need to get entangled in some tiresome postmodern debates about absoluteness/relativity, evolution/creationism, etc. The Christian thrives and ripens on dreams, and the most magnetic dream ever presented is God's dream of "thy kingdom come, thy will be done on Earth, as it is in heaven."

"M" Questions:

(1) Do you think Mark Twain was right? "The only person that likes change is a wet baby." Do you like change? If you yourself don't like change, can you expect your calls for change to be welcomed or applauded? Ought leaders to expect a hostile envi-

ronment when challenging the church to change? Is Walter Bagehot onto something when we said that "One of the greatest pains to human nature is the pain of a new idea."

(2) Ask your church this question: "If you could start again from scratch, would you do it the same way?"

If the answer is "No," as it usually is, the response becomes: "Then, why are you not changing it now?"

(3) The "Hawthorne Effect" was named after a socioeconomic experiment done in 1927 among workers in the Hawthorne Works Factory of the Western Electric Company. Until this experiment, it was thought that only wages and working conditions had direct bearing on work performance and output. This famous experiment proved that increasing the lighting improved work performance. The business world responded with one voice "We need better lighting!" which was logically correct, but not experimentally accurate. It was proven that *decreasing* the lighting also improved performance. In short, what made the difference was not the lighting per se, but the *change* in the lighting that improved performance. For the first time it was evident that social and psychological influences, not just wages, were important in determining worker output.

How many of us need change to improve our performances? What kinds of changes have you made in the past that transformed your life? What changes might you need to make now that can bring you to life? Your church?

(4) Do you think novelist Flannery O'Connor is right when she contends, "You have to make your vision apparent by shock—to the hard of hearing you shout, and for the almost-blind you draw large and startling pictures."[20]

(5) I happen to think that this quote from Max De Pree are some of the wisest words on "vision" ever written: "the real leadership issue is less coming up with a vision than being a carrier of a vision."[21] What do you think? What visions are you viral about?

pART III

tHE cHURCH iN pOSTMODERNITY

tHE eMERGING aND eMERGENT cHURCH

dEAN g. bLEVINS

The term "emergent church" (or "emerging churches") describes a group of relatively new congregations, mainly in the United States and Europe, that reflect new ways of "doing church" in response to our changing world. Primarily a new American evangelical movement, the emergent church emphasizes the ministry of the gospel in postmodern culture. Anchored to the strong sense that God is continually at work in the world, these new congregations provide missionally innovative, organic forms of ministry in their local communities.

While this chapter will attempt to describe emerging churches, defining them can be a struggle for two reasons. First, "emerging" or "emergent" is a term borrowed more from science than theology. "Emergent" describes various complex actions or organisms generating something "new." This new entity becomes more than the sum of its parts.

Emergent churches seem to be something "new." Although they remain organically connected to their culture, they are unique in the way the gospel flows through their ministry. However, many of these communities continue "emerging" (are still in process), so people must wait for them to settle, if at all, to see what their final expressions will be.

Second, definitions often turn people into objects. To be frank, some who identify with the emergent church feel pretty skeptical about a writer profiling them or dissecting their ministry like an insect for a laboratory report. I resonate with this concern and thus will seek to describe more than define.

As a "pioneer" who studies postmodernity, I find that many emergent leaders resemble "natives" in the culture. While the movement risks being reduced to a marketing brand or pushed to settle theological disputes too quickly, emerging churches have a lot to offer. Emerging churches, for all their diversity, engage in conversations, share resources through Web sites and publications, and bear certain "family resemblances" in their postmodern assumptions and church practices.

eMERGENT aS a pOSTMODERN pERSPECTIVE

"Postmodernity" describes a transitory historical period that marks the end of the Enlightenment or modern period's hold on how people think, relate, and value their lives. The term also provides a framework for describing multiple intellectual positions, multicultural engagements, art, economics, education, politics, and value systems. Postmodernity describes almost every new cultural expression in the Western world.

Postmodern culture generally resists regarding abstract, impersonal, or universal concepts as "truth." Instead the culture favors a way of truthful, holistic, living in conversation with the multiple perspectives (both good and bad) that shape our world.

While some people think postmodernity reflects a radically individualistic perspective, individualism really belongs to the final stages of Enlightenment thinking. The modernist view often assumes the world can be reduced to basic elements, controlled, and used for personal success and desire. Postmodern perspectives instead see the world more interconnected, communal, and dynamic.

Postmodernists also challenge any single human definition of reality. They prefer to see how different definitions contribute to a greater sense of understanding. Such a perspective makes abstract claims that attempt to "define" God difficult. However, postmodern natives remain concerned less with "proving" God than they are with seeing how people of faith live their lives trusting a God that cares and guides them.

eMERGING, lIVING cHURCH pRACTICES

Modern churches embrace a set of propositional statements (e.g., articles of faith, a confession, or a creed) that serves as the main gateway into the church. One must "believe" before "becoming" and "behaving" as a Christian.

Emerging churches seem more interested in Christian community and daily living as the beginning point. These churches do not oppose theological or biblical guidance. Often these churches openly discuss core Christian convictions such as the Trinity, listen deeply to biblical accounts of Jesus, and engage in open theological reflection. However, established doctrines do not define them as much as Christian living does.

The emergent emphasis upon living seems to address a culture that is looking to belong first and believe second. Emerging churches attempt to seek and model a Christian way of life as a better approach to defining the church. The baby boomer mantra seemed to say, "Religion is not what you do but who you are." Emerging church practice seems to model the message, "Religion is not what (you say) you are but how you live your life."

Using the term "Christian practice" may sound strange. The terminology describes the intersection between spiritual formation and daily discipleship in most churches. Modern churchgoers tended to see practices as interchangeable or dismiss them as "traditional." For emerging church members, practices carry primary significance.

Emergent Christians tend to see church terms such as "one, holy, catholic and apostolic" as descriptors of Christian practice rather than purely propositional doctrine. Emerging church members might ask, "How do churches embrace oneness through collaboration, model holiness in discipleship, express catholicity in caring fellowship, and express apostolicity in mission to our community?" Beliefs do matter, of course. But "practicing" begins with what the congregation does.

The emphasis on a lived Christianity allows emerging church leaders to recover ancient worship practices. However, emergent leaders blend these practices with contemporary artistic creativity as a means of an authentic and contextualized expression. Worship practices do more than attract bystanders; worship spiritually shapes participants.

Emergent practitioners also place high value on hospitality and conversation. Members often see their church as a "parish." They enter into their local community to provide compassionate care. They open their homes for fellowship. They share transparently about their struggles, as well as God's faithfulness. This "resilient" fellowship allows them to invite people into their communities who think differently. This fellowship allows newcomers to experience the love of Christ before they are expected to share common beliefs.

Sometimes the congregational practices of the emergent church seem awkward. They seem so because emergent Christians often need to "adapt" traditional church programming to a postmodern setting. Over time, however, creative practitioners typically solve this issue with innovative and holistic ministry approaches.

cONCLUSION

Accepting the challenge to live Christianly in the middle of a postmodern culture provides a key insight into the intentionality and authenticity of emergent or emerging church communities. The movement generates incredible energy and hope in the way these communities redemptively engage their world—and ours. One cannot help but be moved by the sincerity and resiliency in these congregations. While still "emerging," these congregations often offer hope for the future.

qUESTIONS

1. What descriptions about emerging churches in a postmodern culture excite you? Why?

2. What descriptions make you nervous? Why?

3. As emerging churches seek to foster conversation about beliefs rather than simply assent to what has been believed, what is both helpful and unhelpful about such a practice?

4. Emerging churches emphasize living more intentionally in community. What are the positive and negative aspects of this?

5. Have you observed the cultural phenomenon of persons looking to belong before they choose to believe? When and where have you seen this? What are the implications for the church?

aPPLICATION

In light of this chapter and its topics, how might you act differently? Think differently? Feel differently? Relate differently?

tHE sENSORY sIDE oF bEING sPIRITUAL

kEITH sCHWANZ

I shuffled forward. In the darkness I took step after tiny step, without seeing where to place my foot. Vaguely aware of a person directly in front of me, I moved slowly. En masse . . . pondering . . . we entered worship.

Once inside, the woman leading the procession held aloft a tall candle. "The light of Christ," she chanted. "Thanks be to God," the response. Three teenagers lit candles from that thin but sufficient light and passed the flame to candles held by the congregation. Darkness vanished.

Few words were spoken as worship began. Few words were needed. The languages beyond words—the language of darkness and light, the language of lumbering pilgrims—reverberated through the silence. We knew in our bones the danger of darkness and the liberty of light.

The rediscovery of the languages beyond words captures postmodern Christians in worship. In doing so, they bust the "contained inside" myth. For them, Christian spirituality cannot be contained and exists as more than an individualistic, interior experience.

bEYOND wORDS

For most of my life, the evangelical church has relied primarily on words in worship. A preacher completed the lengthy sermon, the capstone of worship in pulpit-centered sanctuaries. The preacher dismissed the congregation as if they needed nothing more than words. Sermon structure consisted of three points and a story, as if God could be reduced to conceptual morsels.

Evangelicals' confidence in the precision of words and modernity's inclination to reduce complexities to the smallest components created the false impression that Christian spirituality could be mastered and contained. "It is mine, mine, / blessed be His name,"[1] I sang as a child, an exuberant testimony of personal possession.

The words of worship songs widely used today continue that theme. Sometimes songwriters describe Jesus as a buddy. Even a song that urges the earth to shout and mountains to bow closes with the self-centered claim that all of creation doesn't compare with the promise of God possessed by the singer.

I'm baffled by how we could ever come to the conclusion that we can domesticate God. The psalmist urged worshipers to sing a new song. Why the *new* song? Because God is great (Ps. 96:4). God transcends the human experience. Every day we see new revelation of God's love and mercy. New revelation in the morning prompts a new song in the night. Lelia Morris, a gospel songwriter at the beginning of the twentieth century, got it right: "Had I a thousand tongues to sing / The half could ne'er be told."[2]

The languages beyond words take over when we exhaust the capacity of words. Through space and shadows and colors and gestures and presence and touch, the languages beyond words help return an awareness of the transcendence of God to Christian worship. A growing awareness of the mystery of God invites worshipers to be patient with their own mysteries: paradox . . . doubt. The languages beyond words create space for such reality.

iNTERIOR dECORATING

As the worship service continued, the congregation turned to face the Gospel reader in the center aisle, a spatial sign of Christ among us. Two people held candles nearby: not only is God's word a light (Ps. 119:105), but *the* Word is light (John 1:4). The languages beyond words intensified the Gospel reading.

We knelt for prayer, a gesture of submission to Almighty God. I lingered on my knees, aware anew of this appropriate posture as a follower of Christ. I noticed that some people crossed themselves, touching forehead and chest, physically tracing the cruciform shape of Christian discipleship. Silence followed: aural space in which to know God (Ps. 46:10). We tasted the Communion elements and knew in our guts the goodness of God.

Many in the revivalist tradition have shut their eyes to the languages beyond words—literally. I've been in services where the worship leader urged us to close our eyes and *really* worship." This worship leader implied that Christian spirituality exists supremely as an internal experience. "It's just Jesus and me," some claim.

We become sequestered in other ways. Sometimes worship bands play so loudly that each person stands in sonic isolation, unable to hear the voices of those nearby, let alone the unified voice of the congregation. Or consider a concert of prayer with each person seeming to compete with every other person to be heard by God; everyone prays, but not a corporate prayer.

Take a closer look at what we sing. Many gospel songs from the nineteenth and twentieth centuries and the worship songs from the twenty-first century use "I" and "me" instead of "us" and "we." The ultimate expression of individualism comes when I sing that no other person knows the joy of walking with Jesus in the garden. Or think about this absurdity—if I'm in a worship service and sing that on the Cross Jesus considered me above all else, while at the same moment the person next to me sings it, too, one of us tells a lie condoned by the worship planner.

We have carried the hyperindividualism of modernity into the church. We've become consumers of individual spiritual experiences and an inward-focused spirituality. The motivation of our self-help society and, unfortunately, much of the evangelical church centers on "my interior" decorating projects.

Psalm 96 provides a vastly different perspective. The psalmist commands the heavens to rejoice, the earth to be glad, the sea to resound, and the fields to be jubilant. Biblical spirituality cannot be locked up inside an individual. *All* creation glorifies God—everything created by God and everything created by those imprinted with the *imago Dei*. The transcendent quality of the languages beyond words frees us to see past ourselves to our great God. Multisensory worship busts the myth that Christian spirituality is an inside job.

Many of our Holiness forebears so feared the sensuous that they shut out the sensory. In contrast, postmodern Christians embrace the languages beyond words. They respond to the practices and rhythms of Christian spirituality known before the invention of the printing press and words in boldface type. Much like on the Day of Pentecost, today's multilingual Christians celebrate the grandeur of God through the sensory side of being spiritual.

qUESTIONS

1. What are some dangers of word-only worship or a word-only gospel? Can worship transcend words?

2. Why do most Protestants rely on primarily words for worship?

3. What concerns does a sensory-filled worship raise? How might a sensory-oriented worship be constructed?

4. How much do the words we sing in worship songs matter? What do you notice about most of the songs sung in your church? What is being affirmed?

5. What role should beauty play in Christian living and worship?

aPPLICATION

In light of this chapter and its topics, how might you act differently? Think differently? Feel differently? Relate differently?

wHY oUR (1OVING) pRACTICES mATTER

tERRY fACH

Most people in our culture in the West are nervous about Christianity. For some people, Christianity is considered just one faith among others. But perhaps most distressing are the increasing signs of distrust toward Christians. Growing numbers are spiritually yearning but institutionally alienated. Many see Christianity as a religion of little interest.

Those outside the church often view Christianity as advocating an inert and powerless spirituality that has little relevance for everyday life. Christianity has become a religion that overpromises and underdelivers.

How could this state of affairs come to be?

I believe the answer, at least in part, is that Jesus' core message has largely been lost in contemporary Christianity. Over the past several hundred years, the influence of science and modern philosophy has made the church more concerned with defending the objective truth of its doctrines than with practicing Jesus' way of love.

But I also believe that Christianity has proven itself resilient and self-correcting over the centuries. Today, postmodern expressions of the church are challenging the disembodied holiness of modern faith and recovering essential formational practices from premodern times.

Christianity involves both *a way* and *a creed*. By creed, I mean a set of claims or statements one accepts about the nature of the universe (e.g., that it was created by God). Creeds also offer claims about how God has acted in the universe in various ways (e.g., through taking on fleshly form in Jesus and by sending the Holy Spirit).

But Christianity also offers *a way*—a pattern for living, a set of practices to follow. In fact, in its earliest days the Christian faith was often called "the Way" (Acts 9:2, NLT). Jesus was mainly inviting people to follow his way, his path to God. The earliest accounts of Christian practices include prayer, study, sharing food and fellowship, and the celebration of the Lord's table (Acts 2:41-47).

Jesus described the holy life in practical terms: love for God and love for others. Loving relationships are the sign of the true disciple. As Jesus memorably said, "Your love for one another will prove to the world that you are my disciples" (John 13:35, NLT). Not only that, Jesus says that those who embrace his way of love will be able to do even greater works than he did (14:12).

How can this kind of love be formed in us? The historic answer is this: by spiritual practices that form our souls in the likeness of Christ.

Unfortunately, many contemporary followers of Jesus have been influenced by a modern version of Christianity that places a strong emphasis on inner, private experiences and having correct beliefs about God.

I'm not saying that beliefs and personal experiences do not matter. But what we believe alone is not what matters most. Don't believe me? How many overweight people *know* that being overweight puts them at greater risk of death from stroke and heart disease?

What we want and need is a spiritual way of life that translates the intellectual and the experiential into a whole-life faith. If we are to be formed in the likeness of Christ and become the people we want to become, mere belief is not enough.

John Wesley frequently described holiness as renewal of the whole image of God. Created in the image of God, our goal is to avail ourselves of the Holy Spirit so that Christ's likeness may be formed in us (2 Cor. 3:18).

When we say yes to God, the Holy Spirit breaks the hold of sin in our lives. Our part is to cooperate with divine grace by submitting to a way of life that shapes not just our minds but our hearts and our bodies as well.

Formational practices, such as corporate worship, prayer, fasting, solitude, and works of mercy, are actions within our power that help us become capable of doing things currently beyond our power. In a world of instant gratification, for example, denying ourselves food through fasting teaches us the practice of impulse control. In a world of pretension and self-promotion, sharing our weaknesses and failures with others through confession teaches us humility and reminds us of God's gracious acceptance.

The premodern practice of the spiritual reading of scripture through *lectio divina* helps us to listen to the voice of the Holy Spirit. By allowing head to give way to heart, we are moving beyond information to formation. In this, we can be shaped by what we read.

The good news of Jesus is not a set of beliefs that if accepted will get you into heaven when you die. Rather it is an invitation to a new way of life right now. It is an invitation to participate in God's new community here on earth. This intentional community is called to reveal God's plan to redeem all of creation by its way of life.

In Wesley's view, a holy person is a *whole* person, one whose relationship with God, with other people, and with the natural world is properly expressed. Wesley put it this way: "The Gospel of Christ knows no religion but social, no holiness but social holiness."[1]

If holiness is social, our formation in holiness must be communal as well as individual. Our communal practices must extend beyond ourselves for the sake of all people, especially the poor. And if love is to be perfected in *all* our relationships, our formational practices will also include caring for the environment.

Why do we often lack the power to live and be formed as we ought? I think I know one answer: we're too busy. Jesus invites those who want to follow his way to deny themselves, to leave behind their selfish ambitions and to take up their crosses. The first important act of self-denial for 21st-century followers of Jesus may be to say no to being too busy to be a disciple.

A Christian community that embodies the gospel does not happen by accident. It requires an intentional commitment to *a way of life* capable of standing against the dominant social realities of our world. In the postmodern world, demonstrating the truth of Christianity cannot be left to the philosophers. The plausibility of the gospel demands its faithful practice by the community of Jesus' followers.

qUESTIONS

1. Do you agree that many people are nervous about Christianity or nervous about the actions of "born-again" or "evangelical" Christians?

2. Do you agree that some Christians are more concerned with defending the objective truth of doctrine than with practicing Jesus' way of love? Can you give an example?

3. Do you think that the Church can become more concerned with success and power than self-denial? Can you give an example to augment your view?

4. In what way has being too busy been detrimental to your own attempts to follow God's call and engage in Christian practices?

aPPLICATION

In light of this chapter and its topics, how might you act differently? Think differently? Feel differently? Relate differently?

fROM cOME aND sEE tO gO aND bE

tRANSITIONING tHE cHURCH tHROUGH sERVICE

bRETT i. wILLIAMS

Forget the brutal worship wars of the 1990s. Today the Church is entering another heated debate. This time, however, the stakes are higher than arguments over hymns and choruses, organs and guitars.

In a nutshell, the debate centers on transitioning churches from a *come and see* strategy for ministry to a *go and be* approach. As leaders and congregations make this transition, many claim they are becoming far more unified as Christ-following disciples. And this is what the Church was intended to be.

For the past several decades, most churches have been operating from a *come and see* approach. The goal of this strategy has been to attract people to "the barn"—that is, the church building. Ministry in this model has been done primarily by the clergy or staff, while laypersons sit back and watch. Effectiveness has been measured by crowds and cash, with most of the finances and energy spent by the church reinvested to support events inside the barn.

Countless churches have been planted using this approach. A number have even grown to significant size. Unfortunately, the unintended consequence all too often has been a generation of consumer Christians and a lack of fully devoted followers of Christ. Even Bill Hybels, who championed this approach for many years, now admits that this method is no longer effective. A new approach must take center stage.

What does it mean to *go and be?* Jesus commands us in Matt. 28:19 to "go and make disciples of all the nations" (NLT). This Great Commission is a mandate for the church to *be* missional. Being missional simply means we are to be sent.

God has modeled this commissioning for us in the Trinity. In fact, God's very nature is missional: the Father *sends* the Son to earth; the Father and Son *send* the Holy Spirit; and the Father, Son, and Spirit *send* the Church to be God's hands and feet in the world.

One of the first steps in transitioning a church toward a more missional approach is to create opportunities for everyone to serve. Many pastors are surprised to find a laundry list of people in their congregations who are anxious to discover and then use their strengths and energies in support of God's kingdom. Unfortunately, too many leaders are reluctant to relinquish control over the day-to-day ministries in their churches.

A healthy understanding of biblical diversity may be helpful as we think about what it means to be missional. The apostle Paul uses the metaphor of the human body to make his point. Each body part offers unique strengths, abilities, and gifts that are necessary for a healthy, functioning body (see 1 Cor. 12).

Being missional also challenges the common notion of ministry ownership. In recent years, I have discovered that ministry is easier to transfer to others when their own visions and dreams are integrated into the ministry vision. Pastoral leadership should not monopolize the work of the church. Instead, pastors must equip, empower, and unleash every believer so that God's kingdom may come and God's will may be done on earth as it is in heaven.

It can be tempting for pastors to place people in ministry strictly based on what pastors perceive to be the needs of their church. However, leaders must open their hearts and minds to the idea that everyone has been gifted to do the work of God's kingdom.

In our worshiping community, I have been blessed to mentor a number of volunteers with a desire to learn how to preach. I have been able to empower them to preach in a variety of venues. John Wesley, his followers, and scores of Nazarenes before us have employed this same strategy in the past. We can relearn it.

Leaders must learn to understand that their primary job is to replicate themselves by empowering others. This discovery enabled our worship leader to help us *go and be* the church outside the barn, holding worship gatherings simultaneously in different parts of town. We cannot ever let fear hold us back from seeing the church as a training center to resource, facilitate, and then send disciples. After all, a needy world may not be willing to *come and see.*

I would like to share some examples of laypersons in our church envisioning and implementing new ministries.

The Tennyson Center is a live-in treatment facility where children at risk receive care before transitioning back into their families or foster homes. The dream of Jon, one of our young leaders, was to *go and be* the church to these children. Our congregation has served the Tennyson Center for over a year now by offering soccer and gymnastics clinics, holiday events, and monthly worship services for the children at the Center. Over 150 different volunteers from our church participate in this intergenerational ministry.

The Bake-Out Blessing is the dream of an 80-year-old woman from our church who shared a God-sized vision with me a couple of years ago. Marilynn asked me one day, "What if 50 bakers from our church could bake enough items to distribute to all of the nearby fire departments, police stations, group homes, homeless shelters, and shut-ins? Then the younger adults in our church could deliver those items once a month, no strings attached, in the name of the Lord." Today this vibrant ministry involves over 100 different volunteers every month. Many of these are elderly or have never before served in a traditional church role.

These ministries, envisioned and led by the dreams of volunteers, yet resourced and supported by the staff of the church, are empowering our congregation to *go and be* the Church of Jesus

Christ. When paid ministers believe that every dream and idea must originate with them, our local communities (not to mention our churches) will miss out on the life-changing passions and gifts of the Spirit as expressed by our communities of faith.

As we encourage the Church to serve the world, believers in our churches may begin to unify around a missional vision, regardless of their age or where they are on the modern-postmodern continuum. After all, the harvest is in the fields, not in the barn. Let's move out from the barn, away from the *come and see* model, and learn together to *go and be!*

qUESTIONS

1. Is your congregation more oriented toward a *come and see* approach to ministry, or are you geared more toward the *go and be* model? Can you give examples of your view?

2. What fears need to be addressed by your church's leaders in giving your congregation more permission for ministry?

3. How could your church encourage its leaders to replicate themselves?

4. Pastor Williams reminds us that the harvest is outside the barn. How might God use you to minister outside the walls of your church?

aPPLICATION

In light of this chapter and its topics, how might you act differently? Think differently? Feel differently? Relate differently?

tHE eUCHARIST rENEWS aND rEMAKES tHE cHURCH

bRENT pETERSON

The New Testament witness is clear that Jesus commanded his followers to take the bread and cup in remembrance of him (see 1 Cor. 11:23-26 and Acts 2:41-47). Many in the Wesleyan evangelical tradition have largely ignored both Christ's command and our Wesleyan heritage in sacramentality.

John Wesley encouraged Christians to partake of the Eucharist as often as possible. Today, many Wesleyan evangelicals seem to think that four times a year is a maximum that is seen more as a duty than a transforming encounter. This way of thinking suggests that celebrating the Eucharist is more like an ordinance (following a rule) than a sacrament (a divine-human encounter).

In this essay, I suggest that the Eucharist is the central means of grace for the renewing and remaking of the Church as the Body of Christ. It is not only a chief means of growth in holiness, but the Eucharist is an event, a means by which God heals and empowers, then sends the church into the world to be the broken body and spilled blood *in*, *with*, and *for* God's world.

Some friends and I entered a 62-mile relay in the majestic Sawtooth Mountains of Idaho. Of the six in the relay, only a few had running experience. Six weeks out, my wife and I began to train.

Breathing is something you take for granted, but it becomes central to any runner. Breathing in and out in a steady rhythm helps the runner to run long distances (eventually!). A poor breathing technique will not only cause shortness of breath but also can cause a runner to pass out due to lack of oxygen.

The Early Church understood that life also had a rhythm. It is God's *ruach* (breath or Spirit) that continually breathes life into all things. This *ruach* not only creates but also sustains all that is.

On the Lord's Day God gathers the church by *breathing it in* for communal worship to then be *breathed out* to serve. This rhythm empowers the church to continue the ministry of Jesus Christ. After ministry *in, to,* and *with* the world, God breathes the church back in the following Lord's Day. This rhythm continues to give the church its power, vitality, and vocation.

I have noticed that many churches who adopt the title "postmodern" or "emergent" celebrate the Eucharist more frequently than other churches. I'm quite happy about the increasing role that the Eucharist plays, but I'm concerned that without a robust Eucharistic theology, many will eventually think that celebrating the Eucharist is a dead ritual that "Spirit-anointed" people need not continue.

Let me offer the skeleton of a Eucharistic theology arising from the Wesleyan tradition. This theology affirms that God weekly gathers the church to encounter the Word. The Word is encountered in many ways, including the Scriptures, the sermon, the music, and so on. Prophetic and poetic exhortation inspires this encounter.

The church responds to this encounter with songs of praise, prayers, laments, and the giving of tithes. These tithes and offerings symbolize the willingness of each person in the community to be offered (communally and personally) to God as a living sacrifice.

At the Eucharist table, the pastor leads the congregation in the prayer of great thanksgiving. He or she thanks God for God's mighty acts of salvation throughout history to the present. The pastor specifically offers thanks for the birth, life, death, resurrection, and ascension of Jesus Christ.

Throughout the ages, the church (including Wesley) has prayed that as the bread is broken and the cup offered, the Father would make Jesus Christ powerfully present by the Spirit. The church has also prayed that God would unite each person present to become the one Body of Jesus Christ. In this dynamic encounter between God's gathered people and the intensified presence of Jesus, God renews and remakes the church as the Body of Christ. This joining and empowering occurs not simply between Jesus and each individual but also among the members of the community, uniting them again with each other.

Wesley affirmed that Christ is dynamically and powerfully present at the Eucharist table. He also affirmed that the church offers itself as a living sacrifice in the giving of its prayers, praises and tithes (Rom. 12.1-2). This offering from the church is in response to God gathering the church for a sacramental (deeper and more intentional) encounter.

This Eucharistic moment is a divine-human transforming encounter. In it, the church is continually renewed as the Body of Christ. But it does not end in this sacramental moment. Like any runner will tell you, something inhaled must be exhaled. The church is sent out—exhaled—into the world to be the broken body and shed blood of Christ. This means that it loves and cares for the oppressed, the hopeless, those living in the shadows, and those dying physically and spiritually.

By loving and caring for persons in our world, we are making the Eucharist fruitful. Our response is important for God's love to flourish. Like manna hoarded and not shared, however, we spoil the Eucharist if we do not love and care for those in our world.

The church is sent *in* and *by* God's Spirit into God's world. The church embodies its calling in social justice and compassionate ministry but recognizes it is only able to fully love as it is empowered by the Spirit and sent from the table. The church is *breathed in* to be *breathed out*—to be *breathed in* and *breathed out* repeatedly until Christ comes in final glory.

In all this, the Eucharist becomes the central means of grace for the renewing and remaking of the church as the Body of Christ. The Eucharist provides the means for the church to embody its calling to be Christ's broken body and spilt blood for those who hunger and thirst.

qUESTIONS

1. Of what importance does the Eucharist or Lord's Supper have in your life?

2. How important does celebrating the Eucharist seem to be in your church?

3. What are the most important reasons, in your mind, for why Christians should receive Communion?

4. What is lost or underemphasized when the Church fails to celebrate the Eucharist?

5. Some argue against the frequent celebration of the Eucharist. They say that receiving Communion weekly will make the sacrament less meaningful. Do you agree or disagree? Why?

aPPLICATION

In light of this chapter and its topics, how might you act differently? Think differently? Feel differently? Relate differently?

nOT rEMOTELY cONTROLLED

jAY rICHARD aKKERMAN

Our visual senses are bombarded daily: in grocery stores, airports, restaurants, and even the urban intersections of Tokyo, London, Johannesburg, Toronto, New York—and beyond. Today video screens can be found just about everywhere: in cell phones, mall checkouts, ATMs, automobile dashboards, and even gas pumps.

Many churches are reaching out to visually bombarded postmodern people by using projected videos in worship. Postmodern culture seems more visually attuned, which challenges the church today to learn new ways of expanding its preaching and worship bandwidth beyond the auditory channel.

The move to reach out visually can be especially challenging for preachers who have been trained to connect to the ears far more than the eyes. It is frequently no longer enough for preachers to simply *say* the word. They also need to *show* it for the message to be embraced.

The conversation about how best to communicate is not new to the church. For many centuries prior to the Enlightenment, Christians understood the importance of communicating visually. The prevalence of religious painting, mosaics, sculpture, stained glass, and architecture were in part intended to communicate the biblical story to the illiterate masses. With the advent of the printing press, the spoken and written word became more prominent in the church as ever-increasing numbers of people became literate.

In many corners of our world, the challenge is not illiteracy. Instead, the issue seems to be that a growing number of postmodern people prefer to get their information by means other than the printed page.

What are the implications for the church of this return to the visual?

Those who support the use of electronic visual media cite a number of benefits. "We need to speak today's language," many say.

Others point to younger generations. They believe that postmodern people are somehow more "visual" than their older counterparts.

Still others are more pragmatic, recognizing that visual media in preaching and worship can be helpful to those who are visually challenged, regardless of age.

In a few cases, church leaders confess they have invested in video projectors, computers, and screens simply to keep up with other churches in the community.

All of this leads me to raise some questions. For instance, what happens after a church makes these initial investments? Has anyone considered how electronic media can impact a church's ministry? What kind of ongoing training can be offered? Who will lead this ministry? What are the best ways to convey visually what is spoken and sung each week in worship? How might electronic media shape a worship experience—or even the sermon—differently?

Too often, these kinds of questions are addressed after problems arise. Older and donated equipment fails. Frustrated and/or poorly trained volunteers quit. Or exasperated worshipers tire from media that is distracting, not well designed, or poorly presented.

As an advocate for the use of visual media in ministry, I want to underscore my belief in its ability to convey biblical truth today much in the same way that stained glass did centuries ago. I have seen time and again how sermons visually supported by a dominant biblical metaphor are powerful and dynamic.

But I also know the horror stories associated with visual media. Many times I've witnessed lyrics not displayed in sync with songs, slides coming early or late in a sermon, and video clips not cued correctly. I also have felt nauseated by motion videos swirling in the background, or grown bored by an endless procession of mountain lakes, ocean beaches, and Arizona sunsets. Above all, I'm reminded that electronic visual media offers no hope of making poor preachers good or bad worship planning great.

As a technical media team member myself, I have been stymied by worship leaders who carelessly communicated a list of songs and failed to indicate the precise words that would be sung. Often I have been left wondering who considers which graphics are appropriate to a church's overall worship theme. I've wondered whether a well-meaning layperson who works with PowerPoint on the job is really gifted to assist worship without demonstrating even a basic understanding of aesthetics, religious symbolism, theology, or artistic design. It can be frustrating.

Few of us would argue that worshiping congregations should not sing simply because the musicians are less than stellar. But I sometimes wonder if this argument could apply to electronic visual media. Sometimes I am tempted to wonder if the church should not use visual media at all if we cannot use it well.

Fortunately, a way forward exists that does not require unplugging our projectors and tearing down our screens. Electronic visual media can be powerful if at least two elements are at play: first, worship leaders should seek and attempt to follow the active presence of God when preparing for worship; and second, preachers and worship leaders should seek a biblical metaphor to be the focus of the sermon, worship, and corresponding visual message.

Worship leaders are fortunate that today a multitude of cost-effective resources are available to assist them. A simple Internet search offers abundant links to helpful blogs and high quality imagery legally available for free or at minimal cost. Helpful books, workshops, and support groups exist by which pastors and laypersons can become more adept at communicating visually.

Our bad habits must also be changed. Many pastors need to think differently about their preaching—this time with a visual audience in mind. There is nothing magical about using visual media, of course. Congregations are not remotely controlled by its use. And I don't think that contemporary pastors who want to use visual media effectively should simply hand their sermon manuscripts over to someone at the end of the week and say, "Make it visual."

I propose that the prayerful identification of a visual metaphor from the Bible should be the starting place for all those who preach, lead singing, select music, and design graphics. When coupled with prayer, planning, training, encouragement, and ongoing congregational support, this kind of creative partnership may be incredibly effective in connecting with a visually attuned postmodern culture.

qUESTIONS

1. Do you agree with the notion that if churches do not possess excellent technology, that technology should not be used at all?

2. How have you appreciated the visual elements in worship? How and when are they distracting?

3. What comments of praise or critique should laity offer their pastoral and worship leaders? What training should be offered to church congregations to teach them to worship visually?

4. What are some challenges that face a visually addicted culture?

5. What can be some powerful worship aids beyond PowerPoint? How can more senses be used in worship? Sound, smell, touch, and taste?

aPPLICATION

In light of this chapter and its topics, how might you act differently? Think differently? Feel differently? Relate differently?

cHRISTIAN eDUCATION aND pOSTMODERNISM

mARK mADDIX

Postmodern Christian education is an oxymoron. At least that's conventional wisdom. Christian education is concerned with providing goals and objectives that can be measured. Postmodernism questions the very possibility of such norms.

But maybe conventional wisdom is wrong. Maybe postmodernism can contribute to Christian education. In fact, postmodern ideas and sensibilities may be more helpful for promoting effective Christian education and discipleship in the local church. At least, I think this is so.

One of the Church's primary roles is providing educational opportunities to help people grow in their knowledge of Jesus Christ and their relationship with him. Christian education has historically been concerned with passing on the story of Scripture through the teaching ministry of the Church. Studies show that effective Christian education is holistic, including all aspects of the human person. People grow and develop as they engage in educational ministry opportunities that address the moral, physical, cognitive, social, and faith development of each person.

Much Christian education has been influenced by a modern understanding of teaching and learning. In the modern era, teaching was primarily concerned with the transmission of knowledge from the teacher to the learner. Modern forms of Christian education focused on formal aspects of teaching, such as lecturing and deductive teaching. Christian education in the local church has been influenced by this "schooling" approach to education. This approach has value in some contexts.

Effective postmodern Christian education will require a renovation of current Christian educational ministries to include new avenues of discipleship and Christian formation. In more recent years, education has shifted from a model of transmitting knowledge to more informal, experiential forms of education. Educational approaches have focused more on inductive teaching that engages the student in his or her context. Informal teaching approaches are more student centered, because they focus on the needs of students.

In this postmodern shift, the teacher is more of a facilitator of learning than the transmitter of information. Dialogue and discussion are replacing lecture; transformational learning is replacing knowledge dissemination. Postmodernism has provided a helpful corrective to traditional forms of teaching that were static, individualistic, and lecture oriented.

Christian education in a postmodern context requires Christian educators to redefine their role in the teaching and learning process. Old wineskins must be replaced with new wineskins. Transformational teaching in a postmodern context includes the following characteristics:

1. Learning Communities. Learning communities are characterized by open dialogue and discussion that allows each person to express his or her ideas. The community fosters critical analysis, questions, and diverse voices. The teacher creates space for interaction and encourages each person to engage in the learning process. Some educators have called this "cross-perspectival conversation," because each person lays aside personal preferences and enters into a dialogical community of shared understanding and mutual respect. As the Holy Spirit works in the context of community, truth emerges. Cross perspectivalism provides opportunities for each person to learn from the other in the community.

2. Thinking Context. Effective learning in a postmodern context creates space for critical thinking where the difficult questions can be explored. This kind of learning context includes the tension of paradoxical ideas and unanswered questions. Postmodern Christian education allows struggle and tension, without always providing resolution. It will require much more listening and much less telling. Through this process, transformation and growth take place.

3. Safe Environment. Teaching in a postmodern context includes creating a safe place where each person is valued regardless of past experiences, ideologies, sex, race, and ethnicity. The Church is to be a place of love, acceptance, and tolerance. When a safe ecology is fostered, transformational learning is more likely to take place.

4. Transformation. The primary role of the teacher is to partner with God in transforming the human person into the image and likeness of God. Christian education is more concerned with transformation than information. Effective Christian education in a postmodern context respects the developmental and unique gifts of each person. Modern Christian education focuses on similarities, but postmodern Christian education focuses upon the unique characteristics of learners created in the image and likeness of God. With this emphasis upon diverse uniqueness, opportunities for healing, restoration, and transformation emerge.

These characteristics provide foundational principles necessary in creating an environment for effective Christian formation. These characteristics are reflected in the current Sunday School class I am privileged to attend and at times facilitate. The class is made up of a diverse group of people from diverse walks of life: senior adults and college students, teachers and insurance salespersons, highly educated and relatively uneducated, singles and married, Democrats and Republicans, even Christian and non-Christian. We all have strong beliefs and ideas. But because we have developed a learning community that respects the views of the other, our diversity doesn't divide us. It unites us. Our class discusses difficult issues of theology, faith, culture, politics, and Christian faith. But we do so, believing that the Spirit works in the context of community. We often embody the endeavor encapsulated in the classic Christian phrase "Faith is always seeking understanding."

Christian education in a postmodern context provides a corrective to the modernistic approach to education that is static, individualistic, and lecture oriented. Effective Christian education in a postmodern context creates safe places for people to explore the historical truths of Scripture. And through the guidance and call of the Holy Spirit, Christians experience the transforming power of God's grace. Learning communities that foster cross-perspectival conversation promote opportunities for people to experience and know God in new ways. The result is the transformation of human persons in relationship with God, with others, and themselves as people love God and neighbor. And I submit that this loving transformation is the essence of what it means to be a disciple of Jesus Christ.

qUESTIONS

1. What are examples of effective postmodern Christian education in your local church? What are examples that reflect a more modern approach to Christian education?

2. How does your Sunday School class or small group rate based on the characteristics of postmodern Christian education listed above? What are you doing well? What are you lacking?

3. How do we make the shift from the focus on information to transformation in our teaching?

4. In what ways can we enter into cross-perspectival conversation?

5. What virtues, attitudes, or character traits are needed in cross-perspectival educational communities?

aPPLICATION

In light of this chapter and its topics, how might you act differently? Think differently? Feel differently? Relate differently?

tHE mISSION oF tHE cHURCH

jIM wICKS

As a pastor, I constantly wonder what it means to "be" the Church.

I ask questions that need answers. Could it be that the Church has fallen prey to distraction and sabotage? Could it be that we have settled for what was easy, less expressive, and even law abiding?

Sometimes I wonder if we have been "going" to church for too long. Perhaps we have forgotten that Jesus came to be the living, breathing Incarnation.

I also wonder if we have become more concerned with defending principles, propositions, and presuppositions. Have we forgotten that God is love? Have we forgotten that Jesus called his disciples to live a life of love?

I know I'm sometimes tempted to talk more about the hungry, poor, imprisoned, naked, and sick than actually to do something. I find that many have shirked their responsibility to love their neighbors.

I have come to believe that the Church is in serious need of reordering. John Wesley understood the Church to be present in the midst of society. The love of the Church should attract and draw, offering warmth and light to those in the dark.

The Book of Acts portrays the Church living robustly in God's incarnational mystery. This seems to be Jesus' dream. But I wonder if we have impaired that dream by settling for an understanding of mission that conquers rather than persuades our neighbors. I worry whether we have separated ourselves from the redemptive reordering that Christ dreamed for the Church.

Our English word for church comes from the Greek word *ekklēsia*. This word was originally a political word that meant the calling of the assembly. It represented the collective voice of a body of people.

Jesus seems to think of *church* as a reordering of society in such a way as to represent God's kingdom in the past, present, and future. This representation is collective. It involves the body, not primarily individuals.

Jesus asked his followers to love others, which includes enemies, neighbors, and God. He insisted that his kingdom would be built upon love, and we should become representatives and citizens of God's love.

Love knows no boundaries. Love is unlimited, in the sense that everyone should be a potential recipient of our love. Love extends beyond societal infrastructures, social boundaries, governments, war cannons, truth canons, and neighborhood fences. Love extends even beyond language. It unites and brings walls down. Love feeds children, meets with prisoners, takes medicine to the sick, and humbles the proud. Love unites the intellectual elite with the common folk.

All of this reminds me of an encounter with Wes.

I was paying to park my car when I looked up to see Wes coming out of the mission. I yelled to him with a weird voice that jolted him from a trance.

"What's up, Pastor?" Wes replied.

"What are you doing?" I asked. "Isn't it almost lunchtime?"

Wes walked over to talk. He began to say that he was frustrated and mad. His body language confirmed his words. His head hung down; his face sagged.

This was not the same Wes we had anointed with oil at our Sunday service, the Gathering. We had prayed that God would touch Wes's life and heal him of fear and anxiety. We asked for God's will to be done in light of Wes's preliminary HIV test, which had come back positive.

Our prayer time with Wes at the Gathering was an example of the church—the *ekklēsia*—in action. The people responded to the request for prayer. People came forward to pray with Wes as if they were storming a stronghold. These spiritually young, unique, and eclectic people hustled forward to pray on the floor with their brother in need. They reveled in the opportunity to join in life together.

"Where are you headed?" I asked Wes.

Wes said he was walking toward the riverfront park. The park is a beautiful spot to run, bike, and hang out with family and friends. But it is also a place of temptation. Many head to the park seeking relief through drugs and alcohol. Wes knew I was concerned that he would expose himself to that temptation during this time of darkness and fear.

Wes rejected my invitation to lunch, saying that he was heading to meet a friend in the park. So I invited him to our weekly Bible study. I really wanted him to attend. I knew that surrounded by friends and supported by the Church, Wes would experience the love of Christ he desperately needed

Wes said that he may or may not come to the study. He turned to walk down the stairs toward the park. Wes began to disappear into the rain-soaked streets of downtown.

I thought about the old saying that broad is the road leading to destruction, and many have traveled it. But narrow is the path that leads to life, and few find it (see Matt. 7:13-14).

Something inside checked me. I hustled over to the stairway and called out in a combination of panic, desperation, and truth: "Wes! You got to know that I love you."

Wes responded, "Thanks, Pastor. And I love you."

After a half hour (which seemed like an eternity), Wes came back into the mission cafeteria. He sat and ate. I decided to be patient and wait for another time to talk.

To my excitement, Wes showed up at the Bible study. Before the discussion began, he grabbed my arm and said, "Pastor, I was leaving, you know."

"Yeah, I knew you were," I replied.

He confessed that he intended to see his dealer in the park. "I was gone," said Wes. "But then you yelled, 'I love you!' I tried to forget those words. But they kept ringing around in my head. And I couldn't stop thinking about you and the rest of the Church and all my brothers. It 'messed' me up."

Hearing Wes, I realized the significance of the Word becoming flesh and dwelling among us in ways that I could never have read about, created, or understood. God's mission is to take on flesh—yesterday and today—to make known His incredible love and desire to reorder creation. The mission of the Church is not to just create a place to do ministry. It is to be the flesh of God so that our lives become a portrait to make love visible.

I am eager to live as an intrepid pioneer on the landscape of this postmodern age. I see us, the Church, emerging into this unknown wilderness as the mission, presence, and posture of love.

qUESTIONS

1. The author worries that the Church sometimes settles for what is "easy, less expressive, and even law abiding." Do you worry about this? Can you think of examples that, in your opinion, represent the Church settling for less than what God has asked?

2. Should the church be a political force—in the sense of a body of people acting as God's hands and feet? If so, in what ways?

3. What are the positive and negative aspects of understanding love as central to the Christian message?

4. What do you think it means for the mission of the Church to be incarnational?

5. What about the Church and its mission do you think need reordering?

aPPLICATION

In light of this chapter and its topics, how might you act differently? Think differently? Feel differently? Relate differently?

cRITICAL rESPONSE— sOME cAUTIONS tO rECONCEIVING cHURCH

pHILIP r. hAMNER

It is a pleasure to engage with fellow Christians on such an important subject. No greater question arises for Christians today than to discover the meaning and purpose of the church. Each of the authors in this section has done an excellent job at identifying from very different perspectives many of the challenges facing the Christian church in North America. I say from very different perspectives because each of the articles covers subjects and ideas that vary greatly from the others. In effect, the responses given represent the very point being made about a postmodern context.

Despite the attempt at variety the authors all seem to be pointing to some underlying issues and assumptions that shape the kinds of questions being asked about the church. In the first place I sensed an underlying conviction among the authors that *something is terribly wrong* with the ways in which the church is living out its mission in the world.

Jay Akkerman, Brent Peterson, and Keith Schwanz all see the "something terribly wrong" at work in the worship life of the church. Each of these authors understands worship to be the central uniting practice of the church's life. Akkerman and Schwanz relate the difficulties of the church's identity to the questions of sensory engagement and community identity. They recognize that dividing worship into individualistic practices of devotion serves to frustrate the work of the Spirit in making a new people who see their own lives in the story of God. Furthermore, individualized worship for these two authors serves to cheapen God and his place in the church. This is most importantly expressed in the engagement of the senses, especially the visual sense in worship. As Schwanz notes, "The languages beyond words take over when we exhaust the capacity of words. Through space and shadows and colors and gestures and presence and touch, the languages beyond words help return an awareness of the transcendence of God to Christian worship."

For Peterson the heart of the matter is an inadequate expression of sacramental life. This, too, could be identified as an issue of sensory engagement except that more is at stake in the Lord's Supper than just sensory engagement. Peterson concludes that identity for the Body of Christ is wrapped up in "the weekly encounter with the Spirit at the table. The church is *breathed in* to be *breathed out*—to be *breathed in* and *breathed out* repeatedly until Christ comes in final glory."

Still others of the authors see the "something terribly wrong" having to do with the misguided or misdirected missional practices of the church. We are not speaking about the suppression of unhealthy behaviors of individuals. Rather, as Jim Wicks argues, "Jesus seems to think of *church* as a reordering of society in such a way as to represent God's kingdom in the past, present, and future." This claim by Wicks is really a restatement of John Wesley's purpose for the Methodists. Wesley's claim of Methodist societies (read Wesleyan Christians) was to spread scriptural holiness and reform the nation.

Brett Williams's differentiation between *come and see* and *go and be* churches is a very appropriate criticism of the entertainment bias of too many churches in North America today. Postmodern Christianity has rightly argued against such a self-serving view of Christian faith and practice. It has also argued in favor of a significant reengagement of the unchurched population at the places where they live and work. This is a significant correction in the shape of church practice and the expression of personal faith.

Terry Fach also claims the missional life of the church has begun to find transformation in the postmodern rediscovery of acts of mercy. Using the ancient language of the Way, Fach brings to the front of church mission the loving of God and neighbor. This enables the church to turn away from self-gratifying activities and to the very practices of God's own heart at work in the world.

Lastly, Dean Blevins finds the "something terribly wrong" to have everything to do with the way in which Christians frame their lives in the first place. While attempting to avoid the stark generalizations that postmodernism has come to reject, Blevins shows that the real contrast between a "modern" church and a "postmodern" church is one of abstract, impersonal, and universal concepts of truth versus personal, relational, and concrete expressions of holy love.

The authors we have discussed here have made a great contribution to the further consideration of what it means to be the church in the postmodern context. There are, however, some significant cautions that seem to arise from the conversation thus far.

First, Christians of the postmodern period will fall prey to the same arrogance and pride that has at times overwhelmed other periods in the church if they conclude that their expressions of Christian worship are ultimately more authentic than at other times in history. In other words, postmodern Christians must hold loosely the conviction that their expressions of Christian missional practices are all there is to living a Christlike life.

Another caution for the church comes in the form of priorities, or perhaps more properly preoccupations. The rediscovery of the visual elements of worship are absolutely necessary as a corrective to worship practices of the recent past. This should not be done, however, to the exclusion of the hearing of the gospel. Scripture was heard long before it was read and seen by the early Christian churches. So, hearing the gospel must remain an essential way into the mystery of God's presence with God's people. Having said this, it should also be said that the sensory experiences of corporate worship are not *the* center of worship. At best they are a peripheral issue. That is, sensory experience is not to be worshiped, but the God who raised Jesus from the dead is to be worshiped. Our wired, multimedia culture offers much to the church's corporate life, but it will only be helpful if it does not attempt to become *the* center of what happens in worship.

A third caution for the church is found in what does stand at the heart of the life and mission of the church. Each of the authors in this section is completely committed to a communal life in the church that shapes and transforms the experience of the people. So it is extremely important for the church to recover the priority of word and sacrament as it moves forward in the postmodern context. In hearing the word and then seeing it come alive in sacramental practice, the church is accurately reflecting its experience of the God who is both Other than us and God with us at the same time.

qUESTION

What do you find helpful or unhelpful in this critical response?

26 cONVERSATION iGNITER
rESONANT

LEONARD sWEET

* * *

The soul would have no rainbow
had the eyes no tears.
J. V. Cheney[1]

* * *

The "R" in the MRI Miracle reminds us that the gatekeeper to change is not rational thought so much as emotional resonance. The resonances of emotionally engaging experiences override rational communication every time. People do not so much come to the emotions via the intellect; they come to the intellect via the emotions. It is the blur of emotion that clarifies the blinding light of reason.

If the magnetism of the Big Dream does not resonate emotionally, it will fall flat. That's why an advertising campaign for softdrinks is called "Feel Pepsi," not "Think Pepsi."[2] The moral imagination requires an emotional as well as intellectual resonance and response.

A "head first" Gutenberg world dismissed emotions in favor of the intellect. This helps explain the popularity of music in the modern period: music was a permissible arena for meeting our emotional needs. Even when late Gutenbergers tried to talk about the emotions, they could only couch them in terms of the intellect like "hot cognitions."[3] To advise Googleys to "ignore your feelings," which was a common Gutenberg counsel, is about as smart as putting down I-feel-your-pain appeals or as stupid as trying to have a conversation with a kid with headphones on.

The greatest communicators in history have been those who had the ability to turn thoughts into emotions that move peoples and nations. Good scholars have the power of concentrating into a single image or phrase a world of intense thought. Good poets have the power of concentrating into a single image or phrase a world of intense feeling. Great communicators have a power of concentrating into a single image or speech an intense world of thought and feeling.

In spite of modernity's attempts to deodorize the slime of feeling from every source, alternative voices from the world of the arts and literature—like this one from D. H. Lawrence in 1913—insisted that beauty, truth, and goodness could not be defined rationally, only experienced emotionally: "My great religion is a belief in the blood, the flesh, as being wiser than the intellect. We can go wrong in our minds. But what our blood feels and believes and says, is always true."[4] People need integrated, emotionally engaging experiences. No one wants to live a flat life, a life without echoes, a life that does not resonate.

✽ ✽ ✽

**I would rather feel compunction
than know its definition.**
Thomas à Kempis, *The Imitation of Christ*[5]

✽ ✽ ✽

The decline of "rationalist religion" is one of the characteristic features of a Google world.[6] With the loss of faith in the power of reason comes an openness to the emotions, and to the supra-rational. Evangelism is not helping people cross some rational threshold that panders to our need to calibrate, manipulate, fabricate, magnate.[7] Googleys approach life feelingly, sense things feelingly, and the last thing they want is an unfeeling faith. When it comes to God's presence in their life, Googleys don't want just to know things "in the head"; they want to know things "in the heart." They want to live and love "by heart." And they know that the "heart has reasons that reason knows not of" (Blaise Pascal). The discovery that John Wesley was unsettled as a boy by the attentions of a poltergeist would have scandalized Gutenbergers, but charms Googleys.[8]

In fact, the operation known as "heart bypass" may be a fitting metaphor for one of the key troubles of a Gutenberg world. When you bypass the heart, there is no end of trouble. A primary cause of heart attacks may be the lack of attack hearts—lives trained in deep, hard, attack thinking but suppressed in wide, compassionate, attack feelings that can take on the challenges of life.

For those Gutenbergers whose lives have been spent burrowing in rational furrows and learning to flex logical muscles, all this talk about "emotional intelligence" and "feeling level" and "thinking-feeling" sounds like worthless drivel. To be sure, faith is not an emancipation from thought. Sermons that dull the mind quell the emotions. When you think about it, Nazism was the rationalization and industrialization of an emotion—hatred—and created history's first factories for mass murder. While we must never lose touch with our feelings, we must not always give in to them either. We must be open to the very real possibility that our emotional state may be weird or wonky, since each one of us carries certain cargo that occupies too much space in our emotional life; each of us carries stories of emotional derailments. Every heart has emotional alimony to pay.

❋ ❋ ❋

**If you're going to be convincing, brother,
you've gotta be convinced.
gospel singer Willa Dorsey**

❋ ❋ ❋

No one can make the choice to change *for* you. No one can make the choice to change *but* you. And to choose change is as much an emotional as it is an intellectual decision. If it doesn't "move" you, you won't move. As Jonathan Swift liked to put it, it is useless to attempt to reason a man out of a thing he was never reasoned into.

Ironically, a lot of the research highlighting the "R" in MRI comes from the world of "neuromarketing" and "leadership literature" and not from the church; from people like John Kotter, Daniel Pink, Daniel Goleman, Richard Boyatzis, and so on. Here is Harvard Business School professor and change expert John Kotter providing the background for Virgin Group's CEO Sir Richard Branson's proud redefinition of his title of Chief Executive Officer as Chief Emotional Officer:

> Behavior change happens mostly by speaking to people's feelings. . . . This is true even in organizations that are very focused on analysis and quantitative measurement, even among people who think of themselves as smart in an MBA sense. In highly successful change efforts, people find ways to help others see the problems or solutions in ways that influence emotions, not just thought.[9]

In *Primal Leadership* (2002), Goleman, Boyatzis and McKee argue that the fundamental task of leadership is emotional. Leaders prime "good feeling" in those they lead and to create "resonance," which is defined as "a reservoir of positivity that frees the best in people."[10] In the MRI Miracle, "R" is the "primal dimension" of change because it is both the original and the most important task of leadership: "driving the emotions in a positive direction and clearing the smog created by toxic emotions."[11]

✳ ✳ ✳

**No tears in the writer,
no tears in the reader.**
Robert Frost

✳ ✳ ✳

To move people to the future, you must unleash the emotional power of Christianity. Christians brought a whole new set of emotions and ethics to Roman life.[12] In fact, Christianity greatly increased people's capacity for genuine emotional response.

The gospel doesn't give us many windows into Jesus' personal life. We don't know about Jesus physical appearance, or his social demeanor, or his intellectual life. But we do have lots of windows into his emotional life. His emotional side is explored and expressed on nearly every page of Scripture, and one thing is clear: Jesus was about as far from being Stoic as one could get. Jesus was fully himself, completely authentic. He did little to hide his emotions, to partition off his emotions, or to restrict the full range of emotions at play in his life: from wrath to wrangle, scorn to sneer, rage to rant.

He got angry . . . with Satan, and so forth.

He was easily surprised . . . at the centurion's faith.

He was exasperated . . . with the disciples over and over again.

He was disappointed . . . in Peter.

He was very empathetic . . . with the crowds who skipped meals to follow him.

He could get very teary . . . and cried twice in public, once over a people and another time over a place.

He could get joyful . . . "Why are you not dancing?"

He could cry from anguish . . . "Why have you forsaken me?"

It has always been that just when we started to think that "good leadership" is suppressing the authentic human emotions of frustration, sadness, anger, disappointment, we were confronted with Jesus' interactions that engaged the higher emotions without suppressing the lower ones. Amazingly, emotionologists are now discovering that bringing complex, even contradictory, emotions together ("ambivalence") like Jesus did engenders creativity more than a stable emotional default, even if it's positive.[13]

The cramped poverty of our emotional life contrasts sharply with Jesus' rich emotional states, which tapped deeply into the emotional power of love. What was the worst thing you could do in life? For Christians it was first, the refusal to be loved, and second, the refusal to love. Jesus turned the Hebrew understanding of holiness on its head, and in so doing made discipleship an emotionally expensive calling. Jews could not touch anything that was impure, unclean, or anything that was dead. That was what is meant to be holy . . . to be uninfected by ugliness and sin; to be separate from the sinner; to partition yourself off, as the temple was partitioned off, from all that was dirty and soiled.

Jesus stood that whole understanding of holiness on its head. Jesus could not refrain from touching anything that was impure, unclean, or dead. Jesus touched lepers and others who were "unclean" and in touching them infected them with the love of God. Jesus touched the dead daughter of Jairus and infected her with life. Jesus touched prostitutes and sinners by eating and drinking with them and infected them with forgiveness. Jesus broke the law by letting the "sinner" woman touch him (Luke 7:39) and infected her with hope for her future.

For Jesus nothing is accursed. Holiness is reaching out to touch the unclean, not being afraid of the dust and dirt, and infecting the world with the contagious love of Christ. For it is "And here in the dust and dirt, O HERE,/The lilies of his love appear."[14]

The "R" drives emotions in a missional direction: challenging Gutenbergers to reach out into the "dust and dirt" of Google culture, so that the "lilies of his love" can bud and grow in this new world. Holiness is not separation from, but embodiment in the world. Whatever is unclean, the church has to pick it up, for that is its vocation. When you live in "purity of heart," you see beauty in everyone, you see goodness in everyone, you see truth in everyone, even the most hardened criminal hanging on a cross next to you. Purity of heart is less about not thinking about sex all the time than it is about thinking about God all the time, even while you're having sex. Origen said it best: "holiness is seeing with the eyes of Christ."

The MRI Miracle also requires emotional persuasion and especially an emotional closure that can "mark" the choice of change. Billy Graham was right: for change to be lasting there needs to be a "moment of decision," or more precisely, "moments of decision," and such imprinting moments require emotional appeals and closure. For change to last there needs to be emotional markers, memory that get imprinted not so much by emotional highs as by emotional heights.

✻ ✻ ✻

Instruction may make men learned, but feeling makes them wise.
Bernard of Clairvaux[15]

✻ ✻ ✻

If I were to do an essay on "How Seminaries Lost Their Way," one of the longest sections would be on the de-emotionalization of religious leadership. Preachers are taught to be masters of analytical, critical thought. Preachers are not taught to grow their "emotional intelligence" or to be adept at emotional persuasion, neither of which is taught in seminary at all. Only critical, disciplined, logical argument is. Seminaries don't have a problem with preaching that employs the force of reason, but they do have a problem ("that's manipulative") with preaching that employs the force of emotion. No wonder Gutenberg sermons remembered the head but forgot the heart. Manipulation is using emotion and reason to get people to do things for your benefit. Motivation is using emotion and reason to get people to do things for their benefit or the greater benefit of the gospel.

To reach a Google world, rather than being afraid of strong feelings in preachers, we ought to pursue strong feeling and learn approaches that touch the emotions as much as they deepen understanding. This is where the "R" and the "I" connect, since images appeal to and expand our emotional heritage.[16]

"R" Questions

(1) What "moves" you?

(2) Which would you prefer in an artist? Do you want a sculptor to channel his or her intellectual life into their sculpture? Or do you want them to channel their inner life into their sculpture?

(3) Show the Willow Creek Conference DVD, "This Is Who I Am," produced by Bruce Willems. It's only eight minutes long and features a postmodern girl named Ladonna who speaks to the church about what it means to be a Googley.

iN, wITH, aND fOR tHE wORLD

wHY oTHERS mATTER tO uS

eRIC sEVERSON

Nothing in the universe rivals the complexity, mystery, and wonder of the human face. God's creation can boast of soaring mountains, complex organisms, blazing hot stars, and unforgettable sunsets. But the marvel of these and all the other gems of creation cannot rival the awe inspired in a single human face.

In the face of the other person we find what cannot be possessed, that which resists generalization and categorization. Our models of understanding, which can do us good when we are analyzing the world around us, fail when we stand face-to-face with an "other." In the face of the other we find what hovers beyond complete knowledge.

The tendency is to think that the face of a person is little different from everything else we consider. We think we should be able to categorize and label and generalize people's faces. After all, that's the thing we do to all other things under the sun.

Scripture presses us to see the face of the other person as pivotal for Christian theology. The question of the other person and the importance of the other are among the more important facets of recent discussions about the problems of modernism. A great danger of modern thought relates to our tendency to construct overarching systems of explanation.

The best of modern systems carefully define the role of people and their place in an overall vision of and purpose for the universe. But because theoretical systems begin with abstract ideas and then move to human faces, they risk generalizing and simplifying the radical individuality of the people involved.

The worst systems are obvious in their folly. Racism and sexism, for instance, are supported by bad systems that value one person over another according to ethnicity or gender. At other times the problems with modern systems are sneakier and less obvious. They subtly privilege ideas over people.

Every form of theology finds itself at some point addressing people and their role in the universe. When we develop a tidy way to understand people and believe we can decide which kinds of people and actions are aligned with God's will, we soon are confronted by the lives and faces of people who do not fit our tidy ways.

The Bible offers ample examples of systems that fail to handle people who don't "fit." In Jesus' life and ministry he constantly struggled against systems that expected the Messiah to function as a militant leader, a magician, or a legalistic priest. Sometimes Jesus struggled against the Pharisees and their rejection of his teaching and ministry. As a stranger whose ways were a poor fit for the Pharisaic system, Jesus found himself rejected and ostracized.

One theme shows up repeatedly in the Bible: messengers are rejected and even killed because they bring surprising or unpleasant messages. Wolves come in sheep's clothing; heroes come in rags. In the teachings of Jesus we find repeated reexaminations of the way we approach the faces of the elderly, the poor, the oppressed, and the disabled. These faces are among the easiest to marginalize, set aside, ignore and overlook.

Jesus did not settle for merely reminding his hearers to keep everyone in mind when we think about God and morality. He went one long step further.

In Matt. 25, Jesus unfolds his parable of the sheep and the goats. He uses sheep to tell a story of people who are set apart because of their compassion to people who are hungry, imprisoned, and sick.

The importance of the "other" becomes particularly vivid in this parable. Jesus says, "Whatever you did for one of the least of these brothers of mine, you did for me" (v. 40, NIV).

Who is easier to marginalize and overlook than those who sit in prison? Whose needs are less evident, whose perspective less relevant?

The welfare of the sick and poor and hungry hardly registers on our list of everyday concerns. Yet according to Matt. 25, these are the faces and places where Jesus is found and fed. Here the boundary between God and neighbor blur, and worship blends with charity and compassion. The Messiah appears in the very places we might least expect.

It is ironic that the gospel is built on the arrival of an expected Messiah whom people resisted because he did not meet their expectations. And yet here we find a critical component to the Christian gospel that modern thinking has often failed to consider sufficiently. That component is the truth that the gospel arrives from somewhere outside our expectations, systems, and anticipation.

The unexpected nature of the gospel is not just a first-century phenomenon. It is an ongoing feature of how Christians must face the future and the other. Although we routinely and naturally fear strangers, the place where Christ is found in the world is in the face of the prisoner, the most dangerous and unwelcome of strangers.

In the mystery of the strange and unfamiliar human face is found the gem of revelation. Those who resisted the coming of the stranger—Jesus—found themselves on the wrong side of history.

The questions we face today relate to the level of importance we place on the experiences, needs, and suffering of the faces of those who are a poor fit for society. How important is the stranger, the orphan, the widow, the outcast, the prisoner? How important is the person who finds himself or herself a poor fit for the systems that have dominated the last few centuries?

These questions drive a suspicion that might be named postmodern. Perhaps the face of the other is much more important than the grand, global, systematic tendencies of modern thought have led us to believe. This suspicion translates into a general reluctance to think of theology as working from the big ideas downward, from universal themes toward particular individuals. Instead, we should push to see the way revelation flows to and from the gritty particularity of people and faces.

Perhaps this is precisely the lesson we are to learn from the Incarnation. Perhaps this is the lesson revealed in the Lord of all, who appears in the dirty face of a first-century boy from Nazareth.

qUESTIONS

1. Spend one minute studying your own face or the face of someone in your group. What do you notice?

2. What do you think Jesus looked like? How does what Jesus look like matter?

3. In what ways have we tended to embrace ideas as more important than people?

4. What people groups are most likely to be overlooked in your community? What can you and your church do to address this?

aPPLICATION

In light of this chapter and its topics, how might you act differently? Think differently? Feel differently? Relate differently?

tHE sTRENGTH oF wEAKNESS

bENJI rODES

Seattle's Capitol Hill has long been known as an "anything goes" area. Shortly after moving into the neighborhood, I wandered by a place called Coffee Messiah. It had a large neon cross hanging above its entrance. The word "sanctuary" was scripted on the door frame. And the face of a downcast, thorn-crowned Jesus could be seen through the glass entry door.

I stopped to visit. The owners had painted the coffee shop floor in flames and crafted the interior to look like a cathedral. Behind the counter on a wall of flames hung 40 crucifixes of differing styles. On the large cross in the middle of it all, a Pee-wee Herman doll had been crucified. The Coffee Messiah boldly proclaimed in bright neon: "Caffeine Saves."

After initially being offended, I came to understand that I could not be upset with people who had little idea what they were doing. The owner has never had any real exposure to Jesus. For him, Christianity is simply a religion, a set of ideas. He'd seen the Christian life modeled poorly through a hypocritical, judgmental walk of shame that others call a way of life.

Ultimately, I was haunted by a question that continues to echo in my spirit: "How can we reach people and places like this?"

From what I've seen, postmodern people are disgusted with prejudices, judgments, and compassionless philosophies of life. Many have abandoned our abusive national religion, seeing it as a form without power.

After encountering people with damaging experiences with the religion called Christianity, I came to believe that these people need to experience the goodness and power of God. They need to taste and see God's goodness through the presence of God on earth now, through the Church. The spiritually wounded need a real encounter with Christ and authentic Christians.

The woundedness and darkness present in my community needs an invasion of God's coming kingdom. Complex arguments have certainly not convinced those offended to rethink their experiences with life and faith. The gifts of the Spirit need to be exercised through Christ's unified Body as the Church moves in creative and discerning ways to bring a violent touch of healing and deliverance to this collapsing, comatose populace.

Problems with relativism, homosexuality, drugs, crime, and sex have often made the Church fearful of the surfacing culture with all its poisonous capabilities. Often, Christians live in fear of contracting evil as if it were bacteria.

Yet the reality is that we have been given God's resurrection power to bring about transformation. And the gates of hell will not be able to withstand what the Church sets in motion through the power of the Spirit. We are to live out the kingdom of God— the reign and rule of God—until our neighborhoods mirror the realities of heaven. In God's reign and rule, people are healed of sickness and disease. And everyone can be set free from addictive oppression.

It can be tempting to conclude that we must simply rethink the way we structure our Sunday meetings to "speak the language" of emerging generations. This simplistic approach often overlooks the only hope we have: the power of God. God can certainly inspire our creativity for ministry. But when God's power is as tangible as it was in Jesus' words and actions, it doesn't matter much if we use the latest media or play in tune.

For a season, our church did not have a worship leader for our weekly gathering. We were forced to sing along with a CD. That's not a method you'll find in a church planting handbook! It was humbling to live in perhaps the most artistic neighborhood of the city and yet rely on a CD for worship music. But people weren't coming for a show. They came because they heard God was with us. Our church actually grew during this phase.

We represent Jesus by re-presenting Jesus. And I am coming to the realization that our church must demonstrate God's power through what we say and how we serve. We need a passion for living the Christ life. We need the Spirit's anointing and empowering presence so that we can do good and heal those oppressed by the devil.

The apostle Paul reminds us that he came demonstrating God's power, not with wise words, to ensure the faith of the believer. Our limping generations need to witness the raw power of God through the Church if the Christian faith is to be seriously considered by the religiously injured.

As the kingdom of God is established through the Church operating in God's promised power, it becomes our responsibility to maintain a high degree of holiness and purity. In a narrow sense, holiness simply means remaining undefiled by the world. Yet in its fullness, holiness shapes our lives so we come to live and love like Jesus.

Holiness demands much more from us than merely an individual life change. God also promises to influence us communally. In community we can hear the voice of God, find out what God wants to do, and work with God to send the agents of darkness packing. *This* is social holiness in the best sense of the term.

The life of Jesus is our model. In this postmodern age, we are called to be and do all Jesus extends to us. We are called to believe that God gives us authority and power as we trust deeply in him. Without God, our attempts to create cool worship services are little more than a thin veneer hiding our inadequacies.

My neighborhood needs to be encountered by the soul-bending love of God. It's time once more for Jesus to shock people dizzy and dumbfounded through the obedient sons and daughters of the Most High.

qUESTIONS

1. To what extent are you and your church fearful of the culture surrounding your local church? What does this mean?

2. What can we learn from places like the Coffee Messiah about how people view God, the Church, or us?

3. What weaknesses do you and your church have already that God could leverage as conduits for meaningful contact with broken people?

4. Why are so many followers of Jesus reluctant to express confidence in God's ability to empower them personally and communally?

aPPLICATION

In light of this chapter and its topics, how might you act differently? Think differently? Feel differently? Relate differently?

hOW tO bE a cITIZEN oF tHE kINGDOM oF hEAVEN aND lIVE iN kINGDOMS oF tHIS wORLD

nATHAN r. kERR

A chief hallmark of modernity has been the establishment of political boundaries. Politics, modernists assume, requires that we have a clear sense of who we are. We must know our identity.

A major problem emerges from this view. If politics is all about securing our identity or homeland, it inevitably requires that we make "enemies." We name those as enemies who most threaten our identity. And we enlist "friends" to overcome them.

In the modern era, political sovereignty was about drawing out and securing boundaries or borders. It meant that we identify moments in which the enemy is, in concrete clarity, recognized as our enemy. We name enemies to protect our own identity, and we establish boundaries to become wholly sovereign.

The modern way of doing politics strikes me as blatant idolatry. We should note how far it is from Jesus' command to "love your enemies" (Matt. 5:43-44, NRSV). And modern politics seems miles from the love that makes it possible for us to "be perfect . . . as your heavenly Father is perfect" (v. 48, NRSV).

In the face of the modern politics of boundary making that leads to idolatry, I propose an alternative politics. It is a politics of

155

perfect love. This postmodern politics crosses boundaries and upsets the identities we seek to make for ourselves. It does so for the sake of living "in Christ," to the glory of God. In short, I oppose the politics of idolatry and propose a politics of loving praise.

To articulate a politics of perfect love, we should consider what it means to love *in Christ*. Perhaps the best way to do this is to deal straightforwardly with two New Testament assumptions of what it means to be in Christ.

The first New Testament assumption is that our participation in the love of Christ roots our lives deeply within the reality of Christ's cross. In Christ, we operate at a depth beyond ourselves and beyond our control. This is the true depth of humanity that Christ's passion reveals.

The second assumption is that Christ's love is *itself* a threat to the established kingdoms of this world. Real love is a dangerous and disturbing force. It turns "the world upside down" (Acts 17:6, NRSV). If we receive this liberating love and in turn offer it to the world, Jesus says that the world will hate you (see John 15:18).

To love perfectly is to participate in that same suffering love that led Christians to affirm that Christ was without sin. To love in this way is to refuse to accept the boundaries of this world and barriers between and against people. Perfect love takes forms that the kingdoms of this world recognize as immediately dangerous to their own agendas.

The perfect love of which I speak will likely get us destroyed. This is not a world for love. In the face of such love, the kingdoms of this world go for their guns.

What John Wesley calls "Christian perfection" or "perfect love" names the fact that the Christian's life should be marked by suffering love. For Wesley, such a life is one in which we lose control of ourselves under the great pressure of God's glory. It is a life that begins and ends in praise insofar as it begins and ends in Christ's self-giving love. This is the vision of the kingdom of heaven. This is a vision of a way of life together in which our sacrifice of love for one another occurs as our sacrifice of praise.

Such a vision comes through in Wesley's writings on the Sermon on the Mount. Speaking of the poor in spirit to whom is given the kingdom of heaven, Wesley speaks about a poverty of life that is an abhorrence of the praise of men. It receives life as a gift of praise that can be given to God only.

Wesley affirms the joy of those who mourn. It is a joy that no one takes from you, insofar as it is the joy of hope and the expectation of resurrection. This joy anticipates God's kingdom by participating in Christ's passion.

Our praise happens precisely as we weep with those who are weeping. For in praise, we lose ourselves in the suffering love of Christ. Our loving solidarity with those on whom this world's powers maintain their strongest grip becomes a sign of the one thing that the kingdoms of this world cannot get their hands around and control: the praise of God. Such praise is itself the very political heart of the gospel. And suffering love is the way beyond the modern politics of power and control.

We Christian pilgrims—least of all we wayward Wesleyans— do not have a political identity that we must police and control. We are called simply to love—to love in precisely those kinds of ways that Jesus said would get us killed. To love with the kind of love that, in the face of ongoing economic failure, continues to forgive debts. To love with the kind of love that, in the face of an increasingly violent world, refuses to participate in warfare to secure peace.

This love to which we are called does not try to manage and control the church. It brings infants and the mentally handicapped to the baptistery. It baptizes single mothers and children dying of AIDS in Africa. And it offers the body and blood of Christ to those whom we might not properly count among our number.

To such loving the kingdoms of this world cannot offer consent. But the world itself may, nevertheless, acknowledge this love in praise. In so doing, it gives "glory to your Father in heaven" (Matt. 5:16, NRSV).

The postmodern politics of loving praise that I propose may be the surest sign that we are on our way to becoming citizens of that promised city. We might become citizens of the New Jerusalem, that city whose "firm foundation" goes along with the awareness that here below we have no abiding city (see Heb. 13:14).

Until then, we have no earthly identity to secure, no territory to police, no home.

And such praise is the surest way to be politically postmodern and also faithfully Christian today. For in loving praise the modern boundaries are truly transgressed. And the most modern of logics—the logic of identity—is truly and perfectly ruptured.

qUESTIONS

1. Should Christians be concerned with securing their identities?

2. Can the establishment of borders be a Christian act of love?

3. What does it mean, in the political sphere, to exhibit suffering love?

4. What does the author mean when he says that Christians have no "home" here? Do you agree that the earth is not the Christian's home?

5. In what ways would following the proposal of this chapter change the way Christians approach and engage politics?

aPPLICATION

In light of this chapter and its topics, how might you act differently? Think differently? Feel differently? Relate differently?

pOSTMODERN cHRISTIANS iN gOD'S cREATION

mICHAEL lODAHL

Let's begin with the obvious. When we open our Bibles to page 1, right there in the very beginning, it's about creation: "In the beginning God created the heavens and the earth" (Gen. 1:1, NIV).

Postmodern Christians heed closely the story of God as recited in the Scriptures. And that story's beginning place—the earth on which we stand, the air that we breathe—beckons us to live with deep care for creation's well-being.

Despite the Bible's obvious beginning, there is something about this simple observation that may surprise some. A common assumption is that Christian faith is neither about this earth upon which we depend nor about the atmosphere around and above us from which we receive our breath and our warmth.

And yet that is precisely what "the heavens and the earth" are as mentioned in the Bible's beginning lines. Our Bible begins not in some other world, in some far-off spiritual realm of angels and demons. It begins with the creation of this material world of trees and seas, light and night, moon and monsoon, fish and fowl—"and God saw that it was good" (see vv. 4, 10, 12, 18, 21, and 25, NIV).

The testimony of Gen. 1 to the goodness of creation speaks not of some absolute perfection. It speaks of creation's capability for God's good purposes. All God's creatures coexist to honor their Maker.

This idea, in turn, fits well with one of the most important emphases of postmodern thinking: all creatures, including human ones, live with deep interconnections to one another. All of our relations contribute profoundly to the people we are becoming. In the words of an African proverb, "I am human only because you are human."

The postmodern notion of interconnectedness differs dramatically with modernism's emphasis on the centrality of the individual. And it contrasts with the American context praising the "rugged [male] individual."

Not only does a postmodern understanding of humans emphasize our becoming who we are through our relationships with other people. Postmodernism also says that these profound interconnections extend beyond earth's human communities. This complex web of relations includes all living things, as well as the earth, and the air and sunshine that provide the nutrients for all life.

The Bible describes this beautifully as our being "bound in the bundle of the living under the care of the LORD your God" (1 Sam. 25:29, NRSV). Scripture reminds us that God's "compassion is over all that he has made" (Ps. 145:9, NRSV).

In the era we now identify as modernity, however, this was not the way humans generally thought of themselves. Modern thought drew heavy lines of distinction between humans and the rest of nature. Nature, supposedly, was there for us to exploit through the machines and factories of industry. Philosophers considered nature a slave to be conquered and subdued.

One of the signposts of the end of modernism, though, was the growing realization in the 1960s that humanity's growth of scientific and technological knowledge threatened to destroy most, if not all, living things on God's good green earth. Destruction could come either relatively quickly through nuclear annihilation or more slowly—more painstakingly—through environmental abuse.

A postmodern Christian interpretation of nature, or God's creation, takes a far humbler path than those who wished to conquer and subdue nature. This does not mean that we humans do not have a special role or calling within the realm of God's creation.

We read in Gen. 1 that "God said, 'Let Us make man [*adam*—from the Hebrew word for earth, or soil (*adamah*), by the way, and meaning humanity as a whole] in Our *image*, according to Our *likeness*; and let them rule over the fish of the sea and over the birds of the sky and over the cattle and over all the earth, and over every creeping thing that creeps upon the earth'" (v. 26, NASB, emphases added). All of these, of course, are God's own creatures.

Immediately we should wonder why the Creator is even interested in having earthlings exercise this rule. It is presumably an activity that God could see to easily enough. And yet the wonderful mystery is that God entrusts the care of creation to all humanity, male(s) and female(s).

According to Genesis, then, God has created humans—all human beings, male and female—to *image* God. Humans are to reflect the Creator's goodness in the world and among all creatures. Humans are entrusted with the responsibility to exercise divine rule and care for all other creatures.

Remarkably, this is precisely what John Wesley taught his Methodist followers over two centuries ago. One of his distinctive emphases was upon what he called Christian perfection or entire sanctification. He employed other descriptive phrases for the sanctified life, including "renewal in love" and, very often, "renewal in the image of God." He preached that "the great end of religion is to renew our hearts in the image of God," and that this renewal is possible in this life through Jesus Christ.

It only makes sense that renewal in the image of God would be possible in this life, rather than only in some future, heavenly life. Genesis begins with the creation of this earth and its sky, and then with the entrusting of their loving care and godly rule to humanity as male and female, called to image God. What this means for Christian disciples is that the call to holiness, to a sanctified life, does not uproot us from creation or our responsibility for it. In fact, it thrusts us more deeply into creation. It calls us to image God and be renewed through Jesus Christ, in the power of the sanctifying Spirit, in the divine likeness.

Wesley preached that we humans are called to be "the channel of conveyance" between the Creator and all other creatures. This meant that "all the blessings of God" are intended to "flow through us" to the other creatures. Wesley's basic idea here is that God is love (1 John 4:8, 16), and we receive that "love divine, all loves excelling"[1] through Jesus Christ. We are in turn to reflect and refract that love into the world around us, and to all its creatures.

qUESTIONS

1. What are the implications of the idea that we are all interconnected?

2. The author notes that John Wesley emphasized care for all creation and thought that humans could be renewed in the image of God as they love creatures. What do you think this means?

3. What would it mean to use some of your church's people, property, and resources to show God's love for all creation?

4. What do you think of the idea of people walking, biking, or carpooling to church? Would you be in favor of reserving parking spaces for carpool vehicles and offering bike racks to demonstrate your congregation's desire to be a neighborhood church?

5. Have you ever had people from local utilities conduct an energy audit for your church?

aPPLICATION

In light of this chapter and its topics, how might you act differently? Think differently? Feel differently? Relate differently?

eNTERTAINING aNGELS iN tHE fACE oF iNJUSTICE

bRIAN k. pOSTLEWAIT

Naming injustice in a postmodern world is an act of spiritual discernment. It requires disciples of Jesus to lean into an adventurous life of Christian hospitality in tandem with Heb. 13:2: "Do not neglect to show hospitality to strangers, for by doing that some have entertained angels without knowing it" (NRSV).

Discerning injustice is tricky in our complex, postmodern reality. It assumes that we possess intuitive vision and skilled recognition. In a world often narrated through the historical arrogance of the rising and falling of great powers, we easily slip into self-deception. When we are on the "winning" side of history we are uniquely predisposed to tunnel vision. We rarely second guess ourselves or glance in the rearview mirror at the consequences of winning.

Beware—objects may be closer than they appear.

The good news is that our postmodern lenses often expose our shortsightedness. While some lament the loss of coherent stories that bind us together, others rejoice in their criticism.

North Americans find themselves awkwardly aware that injustice has been selectively named. We rightly named injustice in Hitler's Germany. But we have largely ignored it in the face of Japanese internment camps. We tell a triumphal story of equality, freedom, and justice, but ignore genocidal treatment of native peoples and the enslavement of blacks. We name injustice in the horrific treatment of rogue dictators, yet conveniently justify the systematic, harsh treatment of our own prisoners.

To the degree that North American Christians have named these injustices and ignored others, we stand indicted. Too often we stand on the wrong side of justice.

Generation Xers are my people, and my story fits neatly in the caricatured world of a Douglas Coupland novel. I was born near the end of the Vietnam War and the scandal of Watergate. Still young, my life spans the closure of one world and the dawning of another.

The incubation of generation X goes something like this: we are old enough to remember the fear of nuclear holocaust. We remember MTV before *Reality Bites*. Our minds vividly recall the assassination attempt on Ronald Reagan and the spiraling steam plumes left in the aftermath of the Space Shuttle Challenger disaster. President Reagan's challenge "Mr. Gorbachev, tear down this wall" still rings in our ears. We played cowboys and Indians before it was politically incorrect, and we knew baseball before "roids."

Most importantly, we knew that we were the good guys and that the Soviets were bad—really bad. The world was scary at times, but simpler—maybe not compared to 1950, but simpler nonetheless. As far as we knew there was only one reality, only one story. There was good, and there was evil.

Google? Blackberry? iPod? Denny Crane? Osama bin—who? These realities were beyond our wildest dreams and beneath our deepest fears. For my generation, everything seemed to pivot in 1990 as we found ourselves between two worlds: the waning modern world and the emerging postmodern era. Suddenly our common story opened to a smorgasbord of stories.

My parents never dreamed their son would travel behind the so-called iron curtain as a young adult. Ironically, the people behind that curtain were very different than what I had been led to believe. My puny notions of good and evil, who was in and who was out, melted away. Some of these strangers, a world away, turned out to be angels in disguise.

Of course, we don't have to travel across the globe to encounter alternative worlds. I grew up in a middle-class suburb of Kansas City, and I remember being told to roll up my window and lock my door as we drove downtown. Like many North American cities, Kansas City is divided along racial and socioeconomic lines. At a very young age, I innocently internalized assumptions, stereotypes, and prejudices that were casually passed through my family and community.

Courageously, my youth pastor gathered a group of us once a month for a downtown adventure. We would pick up the Salvation Army mobile soup kitchen and serve hot soup, coffee, and day-old doughnuts to homeless Kansas City citizens. I remember my assumptions and stereotypes withering away as I came to know these strangers, these would-be angels.

As a college student I spent a semester in Washington, D.C., during the dawning of the 104th Congress. Remember the Republican Revolution and the Contract with America? I was an intern with a well-known Christian public policy think tank. They were good people trying to make the world a better place. I was actively involved in researching the debate over welfare reform.

During my time there, an incongruity began to emerge between the policy leanings of the think tank and my on-the-ground experience in this complicated capital city. Washington embodies a tale of two cities: it is a city of glory and of shame, of the powerful and the powerless.

Of the 60-plus staff in the think tank, I was the only person who lived within the city limits. I spent time in a small inner-city church called Community of Hope, a Church of the Nazarene congregation and compassionate ministry center.

In the midst of this beautiful African-American congregation, I was a pale minority of one. But these strangers welcomed me into their homes. Most were relying on faith and hope in the midst of poverty and urban blight.

Inevitably, my two worlds collided. By day I worked alongside those advocating the denial of support to these angels. By night I returned to live in their neighborhood.

The injustice of it all broke my heart.

In 1996, I moved with six other adventurers into a large house in a decaying Kansas City neighborhood. Six of our friends did something similar in San Diego. Together, we founded Kingdom Communities, which are intentional communities committed to a shared way of life centered on the Christian disciplines of simplicity, hospitality, and nonviolence.

Our life together had its share of faith and folly. Many strangers dined at our table and sheltered in our guest beds. Our rich hospitality was like a playful game with serious challenges. At times we were in over our heads. But often we received a surprising blessing from unexpected visitors. We developed lenses to name injustices we did not even know existed. We cried about things we did not know we were called to cry about.

Our lives would never be the same.

Now as a family man with two young kids, my practice of welcoming strangers has changed some. Nevertheless, how I see the world continues to evolve as I meet more unexpected angels.

Without a doubt, hospitality requires intentionality, discipline, and a robust sense of adventure. It can be painful and disconcerting at times. But if we do not entertain angels, we are in danger of developing a kind of spiritual glaucoma that renders us incapable of naming injustice in the world—until it's too late.

qUESTIONS

1. How does the notion of living in an intentional community like Kingdom Communities sound to you? What do you find particularly attractive or especially unappealing about this way of living?

2. What does the author mean by the phrase, "Beware—objects may be closer than they appear?" How could this relate to your life?

3. Some would say that the author's story is a generational narrative: as we grow older, we're not as inclined to take the kind of risks we did earlier in life. Does this seem true? Should this be the norm?

4. Brainstorm with some others about all the ways you and your church might "entertain angels."

aPPLICATION

In light of this chapter and its topics, how might you act differently? Think differently? Feel differently? Relate differently?

sCIENCE aND fAITH iN a pOSTMODERN wORLD

mARK h. mANN

According to modernism, truth is ultimately rational, the world is logically ordered, and the structures of the world are best discerned through observation and disciplined forms of experience. This is what science is all about. Based upon careful observations, scientists develop hypotheses as an explanation for what they observe. They conduct experiments to test these hypotheses. If their hypotheses don't work, they test still others. If those hypotheses do work and consistently hold up over time and continuous experimentation, the hypotheses become substantiated theories.

Science has been very successful in providing useful information about the world. Consider the countless technological innovations of the past century. All are based upon the effectiveness of the scientific method.

In fact, science has been so successful that it came to bolster the modern worldview and gave rise to the belief that science could provide the answers to *all* of our questions about life and the universe. This view is called *scientism*.

In the modern era, many advocates of scientism believed that science could not be integrated with theology or religious faith. The problem, they asserted, is that theology and faith are by definition based upon affirmations that cannot be proven. They are therefore no different from silly superstitions.

Furthermore, many scientific discoveries seemed to contradict claims made in the Bible. For instance, geological and astronomical studies demonstrate that the earth and universe seem to be far older than the Bible indicates. The biological sciences demonstrate that all species—including humans—evolved slowly over countless eons. Again, this seems to contradict the Bible, which at face value seems to tell the story of a six-day creation. Many modern Christians felt forced to make a choice: believe science or the Bible.

Some—in fact, many—Christians today affirm the possibility of integrating science with Scripture and Christian faith. And the rise of postmodernism has helped their efforts at such integration.

Scientists themselves have begun to realize the limitations of their work. Science simply cannot provide answers to every question. It may be good at explaining *how* things in the universe work, but not *why*. Science cannot answer the question of *why* the universe exists at all, why there is something rather than nothing. Nor can it provide answers to questions of ultimate purpose and meaning.

In some cases, science cannot even find answers to the questions it is supposed to answer. Take, for instance, the Heisenberg Uncertainty Principle. According to this basic premise of subatomic physics, the closer one comes to determining the location of an electron (the subatomic particle that orbits the atom's nucleus) the more difficult it becomes to ascertain its speed. Conversely, as one seeks to determine the velocity of an electron, its orbital location becomes more indeterminate. In other words, even when it comes to describing physical reality (which is what the scientific method is supposed to be *really* good at doing), science simply falls short.

If science falls short in these kinds of instances, how can it be a complete proof that, for instance, God does not exist? How can it be the basis for answering questions of ultimate meaning?

This is not to say that science is not useful. Nor am I saying that scientific claims should be ignored. To do so would be to disregard the countless ways that science has been effective at understanding and describing our world and improving our lives. It only means that science provides one (albeit powerful and significant) way of understanding a world. It has inherent limitations, like all perspectives, including theology.

Many scientists also realize that their discipline has important similarities to theology. For instance, both require the use of metaphors—words that give us pictures of a thing but do not fully explain the thing we are describing.

We use metaphors all the time in theology. Without them, we could not speak effectively about the transcendent God. We use words like "rock" and "Father" to talk about God. And we speak of Christ sitting at the "right hand of God." But we know perfectly well that God is neither a stone nor a male and does not have hands.

What we mean is that God is *like* these things in certain respects. God is our rock in the sense that God is a secure foundation for salvation. God is a Father in the sense that God is the loving Source of all creation. Christ's seat at God's right hand means that he has a special relationship of honor and intimacy with the Father.

Scientists also find themselves using metaphorical language. Take for instance a photon of light that can be felt on one's skin on a warm, sunny afternoon. Physicists who study light have found that in certain respects light behaves like a "particle," while in other respects it behaves like a "wave." But they cannot explain how it can be both. They admit that these metaphors describe light but do not fully account for what light really is.

Many scientists have also come to understand that the entire scientific enterprise is based upon faith. Science cannot work, in fact, without making assumptions about reality that cannot be tested.

For instance, the scientific method presumes that an object of study (e.g., the universe) is an ordered whole and is governed by discernable laws and processes. Although this is not a bad assumption, it cannot actually be demonstrated to be the case with certainty. It amounts to a kind of *faith* perspective that serves as a basis for scientific inquiry. And that's similar to the way Christians believe in the existence of God or believe that God has been revealed in Christ. After all, these Christian beliefs cannot be proven with certainty.

What all of this means is that science and theology in the postmodern age have great potential for being brought together in mutually beneficial ways. We Wesleyans believe that Scripture holds the key to the truth about God and the path to a relationship with God. But we also recognize that Scripture does not hold the answers to all questions. We believe that God's truth is also revealed through our individual and communal experiences, which early Christian theologians referred to as God's Book of Nature.

Science is a disciplined form of investigating our experiences. And Christians have nothing to fear from good science, especially science in the postmodern age. Such science recognizes its own limitations and accepts the fact that it doesn't have all the answers.

qUESTIONS

1. To what extent have you or others you know embraced scientism in the past? How does the author "level the playing field" with respect to scientism and faith?

2. Does the author's statement that "Scripture does not hold the answers to all questions" make you feel uncomfortable? Why or why not?

3. How are science and faith similar? How are they unique?

4. Why is science good at explaining *how* things in the universe work but not *why* they work?

5. In what ways might you and your church support efforts to integrate the best of contemporary science and the best of Christian faith?

aPPLICATION

In light of this chapter and its topics, how might you act differently? Think differently? Feel differently? Relate differently?

cRITICAL rESPONSE— sOMETHING oLD, sOMETHING nEW, sOMETHING . . . pOSTMODERN

cARL m. lETH

These six postmodern essays are more helpful in their constructive proposals than in their historical assessments, more useful to inform our exploration of what a Christian postmodernism should move toward than what modernity has been. That is the aspect of this conversation I would like to focus on.

Severson points to the importance of persons. Not just persons in general, but in particular. The bias of modernity toward system needs the corrective of the priority of the human "face."

However, this need not require the rejection of our interest in an "overarching system of explanation" as an innovation of modernity. The West has been interested in a coherent understanding or meaning and reality since—at least—the pre-Socratic philosophers of ancient Greece. Severson employs an overarching standard of meaning when he concludes that those who resist the coming of Jesus find themselves on "the wrong side of history."

The "right" side of history begins in a human face—not, however, in the particularity of "people and faces," but in the particularity of one human face—Jesus Christ. Postmodernity can begin with *this* human face and see all other human faces—and enterprises—through it.

Kerr challenges the idolatry of political identity. The emergence of the modern nation-state has also produced an ideology that can become religious in character. It claims our ultimate identity and loyalty; it defines our boundaries and our priorities. The seduction of Christianity by this ideology is a real and present danger.

This does not require the postmodern rejection of identity, per se. Nor do we need any less to have "a clear sense of who we are." On the contrary, we need a clearer sense of that identity. The problem is not in the notion of identity but its understanding. As Kerr notes, we are to be rooted deeply in the reality of Christ's cross. That central definition of our identity claims our ultimate reality, transcending every other penultimate claim—including national loyalty.

That is the "argument" Paul makes to Philemon and by it he transforms the relation of master and slave. The problems of identity and boundaries are not new "modern" problems, but they come to us in modernity in particularly challenging ways. A clear rootedness in the reality of Christ's cross will help us navigate those challenges in postmodernity.

Lodahl outlines a reconsideration of our relationship with nature as creation. Approaching nature as creation redefines it. And it redefines our relation to it. Our "interconnectedness" is not simply an abstracted notion of relation but our related participation in *God's* creation. It is God's relation to creation that defines the meaning of our relation to it.

As Lodahl outlines, understanding ourselves as interconnected with creation should shape our interaction with it. Stewardship replaces subjugation as the human imperative for nature. Lodahl does not mention it, but the Wesleyan emphasis on the New Creation contributes a creative and developmental dimension to that stewardship. Not mere maintenance caretakers, we are "gardeners" of God's New Creation. That is why "the call to holiness, to a sanctified life, does not uproot us from creation or our responsibility for it, In fact, it thrusts us more deeply into creation."

Postlewait notes the complexity as well as the necessity for engaging injustice in the world. That is true, of course, for modernity as well as postmodernity. Complexity is not a new problem; it just seems to be an increasing one.

We can only applaud Postlewait's personal narrative of discovery and engagement in engaging the problems of injustice. Perhaps it is here that he provides the most helpful model. Postmodernity is less likely to offer easy answers to the challenges of injustice. But we can recognize the problem and engage in the journey.

Such a posture allows room for different journeys and different narratives of engagement. Postlewait's story suggests the Christian public policy think tank he worked for got it "wrong," while he and his coadventurers in their Kingdom Community got it "right." Given the complexity he notes, perhaps a postmodern perspective could call for engagement in the issues of justice, celebrate journeys along the way, and practice humility in the judgment of other journeys along the same way.

Rodes consideration of the social challenges of injustice focuses more directly on the role of the Church. He identifies the call of the Church with the coming Kingdom. The in-breaking Kingdom brings healing and redemptive power, grace and mercy. Our broken world "needs an invasion of God's coming kingdom."

Rodes seems to attribute significant accountability for that brokenness to "our abusive national religion." While we certainly need to consider our responsibility in patterns of brokenness in the world, we hardly need the dysfunction of the church to account for most of that brokenness.

Nevertheless, he is correct in his call for authentic Christians that live out the reality and power of the life of Christ and His kingdom. His "realization that our church must demonstrate God's power through what we say and how we serve" is not new in postmodernity. The early history of the Holiness movement in the United States would also have emphatically affirmed that "we are to live out the kingdom of God—the reign and rule of God—until our neighborhoods mirror the realities of heaven." It is a call we need to remember.

Mann explores the relation of science and faith in a postmodern world. Disillusionment with the adequacy of the metanarrative of rational science and maturing conversations about science as a discipline open new possibilities for constructive engagement and conversation.

It bears noting that the conflict narrative between science and faith was itself largely a product of recent modernity. So when Mann notes that there are Christians "today" who affirm the possibility of constructive engagement with science that should not be understood to mean that this is a new development. The long history of Christian conversation about the natural world indicates the ancient character of these questions and that engagement. Christian faith taking science seriously is not a new phenomenon, but it should be characteristic of the future relation of science and faith.

As Mann points out, recognition of the nature of theological (and biblical) language also helps us in our conversation with science. We speak imperfectly and incompletely. Our language (and our comprehension) is inadequate to perfectly describe Truth. We can point to it. We can speak about the Truth meaningfully. But we cannot reduce it to our capacities for understanding and language.

Our dialogue with science in postmodernity does not require our surrender to the priority of scientific knowledge. Nor does a healthy appreciation of the limitations of our theological understanding allow us to dictate to science. Perhaps postmodernity can allow us to resume a long, engaged conversation that modernity has tended to interrupt.

cONCLUSION

Something old, something new, something borrowed, something . . . postmodern. In this marriage between postmodernity and Wesleyanism it bears noting that—like most young marriages—it offers (expects) new beginnings while tending to underestimate the heritage that brought us here. I have facilitated enough weddings to realize that young couples tend to assume that they are able to start "fresh" and that they will "get this right." Experience usually helps them to discover how profoundly (for both good and bad) they are formed by their background. And eventually they usually come to appreciate that their parents tackled this challenge with similar intentions. In this conversation about Wesleyans and postmodernity it is understandable, but not always accurate or helpful, to assume that we can start "fresh" and that (only) now we will "get this right."

There is very little in these proposals that is really "new." These themes and ideas can readily be found in the long history and conversation of the Church. That is not to say that there is nothing important being said here. It would be an assumption of modernity that significance is a function of novelty. Rather, these ideas and conversations have ongoing importance—particularly given the creative character of this transitional time. The important question at play is not *whether* we will think about these questions (as if for the first time) but *how* we will think about them, and how they will form our living and not just our thinking. This is a worthy and important project, even if it isn't a new one.

One last observation: While the title of this work identifies it as a postmodern and Wesleyan conversation, there is little in these papers that is distinctively Wesleyan. While the ideas are certainly compatible with a Wesleyan perspective, they are not essentially derivative of it. They could as easily be described as postmodern and Christian. And that isn't a bad thing. Nevertheless, it bears noting that there is plenty of room for further conversation exploring more specifically what a distinctively Wesleyan perspective contributes to this dialogue. This is—in a very postmodern sense—a conversation "on the way."

qUESTION

What do you find helpful or unhelpful in this critical response?

cONVERSATION iGNITER iMAGING

lEONARD sWEET

The difficulty of change, and the power of inertia, is reflected in an alarming statistic. Even when patients know their very life hangs in the balance (after a heart attack, stroke, cancer, etc.), the odds are 9 to 1 against that change happening, whether it be stopping drinking or smoking or gambling or overeating or whatever.

There are at least two reasons for this. One is the pressure of family systems to keep people in the status quo. Rabbi Edwin Friedman claimed to spend only 10 percent of his time helping patients to change, and 90 percent of his time helping people who had changed resist the pressure of family members to go back to the old patterns.[1]

The second problem in effecting change is less learning new behaviors as it is letting go of old ones. Cognitive scientists like George Lakoff, Mark Johnson and others have proven that to overcome the inertia of old patterns we need new "frames,"[2] new "mental pictures"[3] or metaphors that can redefine and reinvent how we perceive reality. To change how we live we have to change the frames, or "reframe."[4] Just like you need to "format" your disk, you need to "format" your brain.[5] And that's what metaphors do: reformat.

As befits a book culture, Gutenbergers learned how to parse and exegete words. In fact, images were seen as shallow, without intellectual content, and dangerous. The secure and stable "fixed meaning" of words contrasts sharply with the openness of visual images and metaphors.[6]

In a Google world, the primary cultural currency is image and metaphor. Biologically as well as socially, metaphors are primary and primal. When you dream, what do you dream in? Words? (Some of the Gutenberg Reformers like Martin Luther didn't like dreams for precisely this reason: he said they were all images, no words, and thus sired by Satan). The natural language of the brain is metaphor, which explains why creative children register more dream activity than noncreative ones. Indeed, revelation reaches us in the form of images: these images take form in us from the Word and are incubated in the mind and soul into more complete images that comprise narratives and songs and words.

When you rearrange images in people's minds, when you change frames, you are doing brain surgery. Jesus is without peer in history for "reframing," for shaking people out of old habits and seeing the world afresh in new terms. Jesus' whole ministry can be seen as metaphor surgery—which is soul surgery—replacing one way of looking at God and the world with new mental models. "You have heard it said, but I say" was one of Jesus' favorite segues. What came next? A new frame, which often was an unsettling, upsetting image that was designed to shake things up (e.g., Matt. 10:34). And we wonder why Rabbinic Judaism and the Jesus movement parted company?

The major war going on in the world today is "iconoclash": a war of images. Philosopher Nelson Goodman says that images are more than "world mirroring." They are ways of "worldmaking."[7] You want to change people? Give them a new metaphor. You want to change a church? Reframe your church by giving it new metaphors. A Gutenberger church is concerned about people having a "Christian worldview." A church incarnating the gospel in a Google world is more concerned about narrative identity than "worldview." We all think narratively, which is where we form our worldviews anyway.

The ultimate "proof" is: who tells the better story; who conceives the better metaphors. Give someone a task, and you change their life—for a day. Give someone a metaphor that wraps a story, and you change their life—for a lifetime. To change behavior we must change the frames, and it is images that do the "framing."

This is why an increasing number of churches are using artists and poets as image consultants and "imagesmiths."[8] I even know of one church who has a "metaphorist" as a part of the pastoral team.

✳ ✳ ✳

World's Biggest Metaphor Hits Ice-Berg
The Onion's headline on the *Titanic*[9]

✳ ✳ ✳

So powerful are "pictures" that W. J. T. Mitchell treats images as living things—"image-as-organism"—that have a life of their own and make demands on us.[10] In fact, Mitchell says that the question is less one of "what do pictures mean" than "what do pictures want," and "what do we want from pictures?"[11] If images are potentially much more redemptive than words, they can also be much more destructive. Many of our current metaphors of the church are preventing the church from being the church. I call these souljacking metaphors that steal the soul of the church "Killer Metaphors."

If a couple hundred thousand people die a year from medical error (iatrogenic illnesses), thousands of churches die each year from an ecclesial form of iatrogenic illness: bad metaphors, bad frames. Here may be the No. 1 metaphor that is killing the church: "harbor" or "refuge." Does your church see itself as a retreat from the world, or as a vanguard of God's dream for the world? Or what about the church as a place where you are "fed," and your needs are met?

If the church exists to spoon-feed people, you will spend all your time dealing with complaints about "bad food." When M. G. Johnson hears people say, "I go to church to be fed," he usually tells them, "Then you'll end up a junk food junkie!"

It is important to remember three things about metaphors. First, every metaphor breaks down. There comes a time when to push a metaphor any further is to falsify the truth. Second, metaphors do not exist apart from communal relationships. They are by nature interactive, and thus need to be contextualized and homegrown in native soil. Third, not everything is a metaphor. Some things are not metaphorical. God does not conform to our images. Jesus' death and resurrection was not metaphorical then, and it is not metaphorical now. The fact that Jesus wants to live his resurrection life in you and me is not some satisfying metaphor. It is the hard essence of gospel truth.

cONCLUSION:

It has been said that there are two kinds of people in this world: those who build dams, and those who build bridges. If we strive not to be a dam church but a bridge church to the Google world that is coming to life around us, we must learn to do Magnetic Resonant Imaging (MRI).

But each component of the MRI Miracle is a feedback loop to the other. For example, emotional engagement feeds back into images, which then enable the magnetism of a big dream to shine. And the more images we create, the better our emotional life and the higher-up our relationships. A love letter that describes the beloved as a . . . . may be factual and accurate, but it will not inspire marriage.

But even when we build MRI bridges to this Google world; even when we deploy M and R and I to their fullest degree: we lack one thing.

Only God can truly change the human heart.

"I" Questions

(1) Lakoff says that frames are part of the "cognitive unconscious," but the way we know "what our frames are, or evoke new ones, springs from language."[12] Discuss more the interplay of words and images, propositions and metaphors.

(2) Assess the differences in the metaphors of "ladder" and "wheel," as reflected in "We are Climbing Jacob's Ladder" vs. "Ezekiel Got a Wheel." Is one metaphor more generative and relevant than the other, or are both equally valuable depending on the context?

(3) We are all summoned to be a living metaphor. Is it possible for Christians to be anything but a mixed metaphor?

(4) What Gutenberg metaphors no longer reference a world that anyone understands or wants. How prevalent do you think the exhaustion of metaphors is in the church? In what ways was the Protestant Reformation a revolution in metaphors?

(5) How much of a magical relation is there between an image and what it represents?

You don't think a picture or image casts a spell?

Take out a picture of someone you love—your child, your mother, your spouse. Now, cut out the eyes from the picture. Can you do it? How do you feel now?[13]

To what extent does critique and deconstruction break the spell of the image? Do you think we need to teach our kids to critique and deconstruct some images, so that their spell over life can be broken? What might some of those images be?

(6) If you are "missing something," it is probably because you don't "get the picture." Does your church "Get the Picture"? I know you have a "Mission Statement." What's your "Image Statement"?

(7) Give some examples of Jesus' reframing. Here is one example to get you started: Jesus reframed the Hebrew conception of Shema (morality and justice) with perceptions of "Love your enemies," "Go the second mile," "Return good for evil," "Forgive 70x7."

(8) Check out how postmodern artist Chris Jordan is "Running the Numbers" in his art at www.chrisjordan.com. Jordan takes the dry language of statistics of our mass consumption and turns them into images that we can see. How many cell phones do we throw away A DAY? He shows an image of that stat. 60,000 paper bags is the number of bags we use in the U.S. in 5 seconds. So he shows 5 seconds of bags, or one minute's worth of plastic bag use. He calls this "Intolerable Beauty."

cONCLUDING eSSAY
a rESPONSE tO
pOSTMODERN aND
wESLEYAN?

dAVID j. fELTER

gENERAL eDITOR, cHURCH oF tHE nAZARENE

Most of us love what's new. Some of my fondest memories of childhood were those times my father would allow me to accompany him to the automobile dealerships when new cars were put on display. In those days long ago, it was a rite of passage for men every fall to visit the showrooms and look at the new cars. There is just something special about the smell of a new car. One ride around the block in one of those new cars just made riding in the family car that much more tasteless. The bells and whistles, to say nothing of the increase in horsepower and the new chrome trim, made last year's models look simply old-fashioned.

Postmodernism is one of those wonderful new ideas, on display in the showroom of philosophy. Proponents of this newly coined zeitgeist are quick to point out the new features that simply make modernity old hat. In partnership with them are theologians and philosophers that truly believe that the Church must somehow find ways to accommodate this newly defined essence so that new words and terms can be included in our vocabularies to demonstrate how compatible our present theology is with the spirit of the age.

It is simply not fitting for those of us who are in the pastoral tradition to indulge in obscurantism by decrying the inexorable advance of the new! Tenaciously clinging to old shibboleths is akin to using outdated similes and metaphors in an attempt to establish connections across generational chasms. Unfortunately, many attempts to step into the middle of a fast-moving current result in difficulty. Those who seek to question the claims of postmodernism and the efforts of theologians to reconcile it with Wesleyan theology may risk being perceived as obscurantist. This is a risk, however, that we must take if we are to be faithful to our understanding, experience, and worldview.

This text provides several opportunities to open a dialogue between several groups within the Church:

1. The proponents of postmodernism.
2. The observers of postmodernism who are quite sure that it's the new game in town for the Church.
3. Those of us who are often labeled as traditionalists because we are a bit unsure of the possibility of a neat and tidy fit between postmodernism and the Wesleyan perspective of the scriptural message.
4. Clearly there is another group with whom dialog is possible; those who believe that postmodernism and Wesleyanism are such good dance partners that a marriage can't be too far off.

When closely examining the slippery tenants of postmodernism, there are several essential elements that "stress" traditional Wesleyan perspectives. These are articulately identified by Scott Daniels and Thomas Jay Oord. Further reflection suggests this conversation has relevance to these and perhaps other questions:

1. What does postmodern Wesleyanism say about truth?
2. What does postmodern Wesleyanism say about the Scriptures?
3. What does postmodern Wesleyanism say about God as Creator?

An important ancillary to this discussion concerns the whole issue of truth. Thomas Jay Oord places this issue in bold relief. As I read this material, a nagging question continually surfaced: are the authors suggesting a relativistic, relational emphasis on experience rather than the bedrock of received truth? If so, such a premise makes *experience* the foundation on which all truth claims must rest. This makes all truth claims to be rooted in the perceived value of personal experience. One can quickly see how such an argument can lead to philosophical as well as practical relativism. All truth claims, according to this model, are situated on the shifting sands of personal experience rather than the received truth of God's revelatory disclosure. David Wilson, general secretary, Church of the Nazarene, describes this phenomenon as transforming the Wesleyan quadrilateral into a unilateral, that is, experience becomes the only leg of what was once a four-legged stool.

Gerard Reed and Carl Leth have eloquently articulated the issues that surround this topic. Postmodern Wesleyanism might even be an oxymoron. John and Charles Wesley were not nearly so relativistic as some would suppose. Neither did they understand prevenient grace as the common denominator that mediates some kind of universal salvation simply by virtue of its ubiquitous presence.

Indeed, these two brothers possessed a clear understanding of the role of God as Creator of the world. Wesley reminded the world that he wished to be known as a "man of one book"! Because there is so much to say on this topic, it is important for us to hear this dialogue. It is imperative, however, that we not jettison the scripturally informed positions, convictions, and commitments the holiness churches have derived from their careful study of John Wesley.

Clearly, it is important for the Wesleyan movement to understand the terminologies used in any discussion of truth. Truth is essential to the Wesleyan theological position. Thus, it is incumbent upon religious thinkers to accurately understand what is really being said about the nature of truth from a postmodern perspective.

Often our best generalizations, when read in the cold, hard light of reality, seem confusing. Our best efforts at summarizing often leave us with only a shorthand code that economically expresses our initial thoughts, while leaving untouched the deepest strata of truth.

There is much that is commendable in this text. The energizing syntax of Leonard Sweet's contribution utilizes clever turns of speech that communicate a grand optimism that is at the heart of Wesleyanism. As I pondered the intricacies of Sweet's verbal canvas, I was struck once again by the hope of the gospel and the facilitating grace our Wesleyan perspective offers in its proclamation and incarnation. Indeed, it is my conviction that God has given the Church a great gift in the Wesleyan tradition of which we are the heirs as well as stewards of its richness.

The gospel stands firm like a rock against which beat the vagaries of culture, philosophy, and even religion. My sense of caution when examining any cultural or philosophical domain or category demands that I begin first with the gospel and then look for the synapses of grace that bridge from offer and provision, to experience. I commend my colleagues for their work and pray that God will continue to stimulate our inquiry as we live out the claims of the gospel.

aCKNOWLEDGMENTS

Many people contributed to making this book a reality. We especially thank the chapter contributors, those who wrote endorsements, and preface writers Nina Gunter and Jesse Middendorf. We are grateful to those who wrote critical responses and to Len Sweet for offering his insightful comments.

We also want to thank those involved in the "nuts and bolts" of carrying this project through to completion. We thank Richard Buckner, Bonnie Perry, Barry Russell, and David Felter.

We did a test run of this book with members of Mark Maddix's Faith and Culture class at Nampa First Church of the Nazarene. We thank the following for being part of that process: Kim Akkerman, Stephanie Bartlow, Dan Bechtold, Holly Beech, Jake Bodenstab, Nikki Bodenstab, Darlene Brasch, John Brasch, Rebecca Clark, Carey Cook, Tracey Cook, Dean Cowles, Cassandra Crosland, Brad Daniels, Christy Daniels, Steen Edwards, Anne Edwards, Natalie Elliston, Jodie Engel, Steve Engel, Lisa Fesenbek, Brian Freiburghaus, Stacy Freiburghaus, Jordan Freiburghaus, Ben Gall, Rachel Gall, Jennifer Groves, Geoff Groves, Lia Hardy, Stacy Harmon, Taylor Hauck, Jane Henry, Bob Henry, Peter Johnson, Marci Kielman, Rob Kielman, Deanna Kinsman, Paul Kinsman, Rich Koehler, Lindsay Kuhl, Steve Kuhl, Beverly Laird, Irving Laird, Sara Lawson, Jessica Lewis, Chadwick Lewis-Fridley, Rachel Lund, Mark Maddix, Sherri Maddix, Bradon McDaniel, Steve McHargue, Janee Mestrovich, Allea Meza, Grant Miller, Deborah Miller, Roger Miller, Kathrena Mountjoy, Steve Mountjoy, Jeffrey Nicol, Malloree Norris, Naomi O'Hare, Cheryl Oord, Lexi Oord, Louise Oord, Sydnee Oord, Joe Pearson, Karen Pearson, Kylee Pearson, Anne Peterson, Lance Pounds, Lacey Smith, Tricia Snyder, Chris Spicer, Craig Stensgaard, LeAnn Stensgaard, Faith Stewart, Emily Strickler, Libby Tedder, Annette Thompson, Richard Thompson, Sarah Thompson, Alex VanOeveren, Kylee Vienna, Mitch Ward, Rachel Ward, Verne Ward IV.

Others who deserve a word of appreciation include Kent Conrad, Jill Jones, Malloree Norris.

We also acknowledge those who have been our critics over recent years. Although we may never fully agree, we hope that we can still share our hearts and hands in service. As Wesleyans, we pray that we can affirm each other as brothers and sisters in Christ even as we disagree on what ideas may best support our Christian convictions.

Finally, we are always indebted to the near and dear—our families. We thank Kim, Parker, Hailey, and Lauren Akkerman; Cheryl, Andee, Lexi, and Sydnee Oord; and Anne, Alexis, and Noah Peterson.

nOTES

Chapter 2
    1. *Manual, Church of the Nazarene, 2005-2009* (Kansas City: Nazarene Publishing House, 2005), 7.

Chapter 7
    1. George Orwell, *Nineteen Eighty-Four, A Novel* (New York: Harcourt, Brace & Co., 1949).
    2. Arnold J. Toynbee, *A Study of History,* 12 vols. (London and New York: Oxford University Press, 1948-61).
    3. Peggy McIntosh, "White Privilege: Unpacking the Invisible Knapsack," in *Peace and Freedom* (July/August 1989): 10-12.
    4. Thomas Aquinas, *Quaestiones Disputatae de Veritate.*
    5. Pope Paul VI, "Dogmatic Constitution on Divine Revelation—*Dei Verbum"* (1965).

Chapter 8
    1. Anthony Russell, *The Country Parish* (London: SPCK, 1986), 63, 103.
    2. Matthew Arnold, "Stanzas from the Grande Chartreuse," in *The Works of Matthew Arnold* (Hertfordshire, England: Ware, Wordsworth, 1995), 272.
    3. For other scholars shying away from the "postmodern" language, see Brian Leiter's *The Future for Philosophy* (Oxford: Oxford University Press, 2005): "postmodernism is nonexistent in all the leading philosophy departments throughout the English-speaking world, where it is regarded, with justice, as sophomoric skeptical posturing."
    4. The Religions of Ancient Israel: A Synthesis of Parallactic Approaches [Continuum]
    5. Quoted by John H. Schaar, *Escape from Authority: Perspectives of Erich Fromm* (New York: Basic Books, 1961), 289.

Chapter 13
    1. Brian D. McLaren, *A New Kind of Christian* (San Francisco: Jossey-Bass, 2001), 48.

Chapter 14
    1. Oprah Winfrey, "What Is Christ-Consciousness?" http://www.oprah.com/community/thread/34562.
    2. George F. Regas, "Interpreting Christ in a Pluralistic World," sermon at All Saints Church, Pasadena, Calif., April 28, 2002.

Chapter 16
    1. Gaia Vince, "The Many Ages of Man," *NewScientist,* 17 June 2006, 50-53.
    2. W. J. Thomas Mitchell, *What Do Pictures Want? The Lives and Loves of Images* (Chicago: University of Chicago Press, 2005), 52.
    3. Adin Steinsaltz, *On Being Free* (Northvale, N.J.: Jason Aronson, 1995), 210.
    4. This is the concluding phrase of Eric Hobsbawm, *Age of Extremes: A History of the World, 1914-1991* (New York: Pantheon Books, 1994), 585.

5. Carl G. Jung, *Mysterium Coniunctionis: An Enquiry into the Separation and Synthesis of Psychic Opposites in Alchemy*, trans. R. F. C. Hull, Bollingen series xx, (New York: Pantheon Books, 1963), 358.

6. As quoted in James J. Bacik, *The Gracious Mystery: Finding God in Ordinary Experience* (Cincinnati: St. Anthony Messenger Press, 1987), 60.

7. Ever since it was published in 1998, I have recommended a strange resource as "required reading" for all preachers: Edwin Schlossberg's *Interactive Excellence.* I now have another even stranger recommendation as "required reading" for all preachers: a cover article entitled "Change or Die" from the business magazine *Fast Company* by one of its senior editors, Alan Deutschman (May 2005, 54-61), www.fastcompany.com/magazine/94/open_change-or-die.html.

8. Alan Deutschman, "Change or Die," *Fast Company*, May 2005, 60, 53-61, http://www.fastcompany.com/magazine/94/open_change-or-die.html (accessed 27 December 2005).

9. Ibid.

10. Ibid.

11. Quoted in "Principle 7: Strategic Consumption," Worldchanging, May 14, 2007, http://www.worldchanging.com/archives/006693.html (accessed 30 April 2009).

12. Thought of Daniel Burnham in a paper read before the Town Planning Conference, London, 1910. The exact words are reconstructed by Willis Polk, Burnham's partner. See Henry H. Saylor, "Make No Little Plans," *Journal of the American Institute of Architects*, March 1957): 95. See also Charles Moore, *Daniel Burnham* (Boston: Houghton-Mifflin, 1921), 2:147, where the full quote is: "Make no little plans; they have no magic to stir men's blood and probably their selves will not be realized. Make big plans, aim high in hope and work, remembering that a nobel logical diagram once recorded will never die, but long after we are gone will be a living thing, asserting itself with ever growing insistency. Remember that our sons and grandsons are going to do things that would stagger us. Let your watchword be order and your beacon beauty."

13. The first instance of science fiction in Western culture was Johanes Kepler's *Somnium* ("Dream"), published after his death in 1634.

14. 1 Thess. 4:9-12, author's paraphrase.

15. Luke 19:3, author's paraphrase.

16. What Goethe actually said is this:

Enough words have been exchanged;
Now at last let me see some deeds!
While you turn compliments,
Something useful should transpire.
What use is it to speak of inspiration?
To the hesitant it never appears.
If you would be a poet,
Then take command of poetry.
You know what we require,
We want to down strong brew;
So get on with it!
What does not happen today, will not be done tomorrow,
And you should not let a day slip by,
Let resolution grasp what's possible
And seize it boldly by the hair;
It will not get away
And it labors on, because it must.

—Johann Wolfgang von Goethe, "Prologue in the Theater,"
Manager speaks, Faust I, Zeilen 214-30.

17. See Abba Eban's famous line about the Palestininans—they "never pass up an opportunity to pass up an opportunity." Quoted in Edward T. Oakes, "Discovering the American Aristotle," *First Things* 38(December 1993):25, http://www.firstthings.com/ftissues/ft9312/articles/oakes.html (accessed 27 December 2005).

18. Stuart Murray, preface to *Post-Christendom* (Carlisle, UK: Paternoster Press, 2004), *xv.*

19. This is perhaps the No. 1 mistake of curators: placing the collection's largest pictures in spaces that are too wide or too high.

20. Flannery O'Connor, "The Fiction Writer and His Country," in *Mystery and Manners: Occasional Prose,* selected and ed. Sally and Robert Fitzgerald (New York: Farrar, Straus, & Giroux, 1969), 34.

21. Max De Pree, "How to Create a Lively and Harmonious Future," *Leadership,* Summer 1994, 18.

Chapter 18

1. Elisha Hoffman, "It Is Mine" in *Sing to the Lord* (Kansas City: Lillenas Publishing Co., 1993), 414.

2. Lelia N. Morris, "Let All the People Praise" in *Sing to the Lord,* 61.

Chapter 19

1. John Wesley, "Preface to 1739 Hymns and Sacred Poems" in The Works of John Wesley, ed. Jackson (Kansas City: Beacon Hill Press of Kansas City, 1978), 14:321.

Chapter 26

1. John Vance Cheney, "Tears," *The Century,* 44:4 (August 1892), 538. Thanks to Alan Jamieson, *Journeying in Faith: In and Beyond the Tough Places* (London: SPCK, 2004), 154, for first introducing me to this quote.

2. Check out the work of Christopher Nold, a cartographer of the emotions. Nold is building an emotional map of the planet, a holistic emotional landscape of cities that shows daily where people are most engaged, most enraged, and so on.

3. Alister McGrath with Joanna Collicutt McGrath, *The Dawkins Delusion? Atheistic Fundamentalism and the Denial of the Divine.*

4. D. H. Lawrence, "To Ernest Collings, 17 January 1913," in *The Letters of D. H. Lawrence,* ed. James T. Boulton (New York: Cambridge University Press, 1979), 1:503.

5. *The Imitation of Christ,* trans. R. Challoner (Dublin 1915), 3.

6. For a superb analysis of this, see Heath White, *Postmodernism 101,* pp. 81-92. "Emotion and the vehicles that produce it, like pictures, films stories, plays and poems, are not necessarily any less reliable, and are possibly more powerful, than logic and its vehicles, such as editorials, philosophical theories, sermons, or treatises of systematic theology. So, for instance, a sermon from Romans on the difference between the man under law and the man under grace may not make much impact, but a story illustrating the difference, like *Les Miserables,* might make an impression."

7. The 4th-century theologian and bishop of Constantinople St. John Chrysostom blamed "the dust-cloud of countless reasonings" unrestrained by the "voice of the Spirit" for heretical trends in the church. The exact quote is as follows: "For being ashamed to allow of faith, and to seem ignorant of heavenly things, they involve themselves in the dust-cloud of countless reasonings." See *The Homilies of St. John Chrysostom on the Epistle of St. Paul the Apostle to the Romans,* trans. J. B. Mor-

ris and W. H. Simcox, rev. George B. Stevens, in *A Select Library of the Nicene and Post-Nicene Fathers of the Christian Church*, ed. Philip Schaff (New York: Christian Literature, 1889), 11:349-50.

8. For more see Una McGovern, ed., *Chambers Dictionary of the Unexplained* (Edinburgh: Chambers, 2008).

9. Alan Deutschman, "Change or Die," *Fast Company*, May 2005, 55, http://www.fastcompany.com/magazine/94/open_change-or-die.html (accessed 27 December 2005).

10. Daniel Goleman, Richard Boyatzis, Annie McKee, *Primal Leadership: Realizing the Power of Emotional Intelligence* (Boston: Harvard Business School Press, 2002), ix; also published in paperback as *Primal Leadership: Learning to Lead with Emotional Intelligence* (Boston: Harvard Business School Press, 2004).

11. Ibid., 5.

12. For what the emotional life that preceded Christianity was like, see Robert A. Kaster, *Emotion, Restraint, and Community in Ancient Rome: Classical Culture and Society* (New York: Oxford University Press, 2006).

13. Lindsey Gerdes, "The Power of Ambivalent Thinking," *BusinessWeek*, 30 October 2006, 16.

14. Henry Vaughan, "The Revival," *The Complete Poems* (London: Oxford University Press, 1963), 370.

15. Quoted in John Cottingham, *On the Meaning of Life* (New York: Routledge, 2003), 100.

16. For more of this see Daniel Goleman, Richard Boyatzis, Annie McKee, *Primal Leadership*.

Chapter 30

1. Charles Wesley, "Love Divine, All Loves Excelling" in *Sing to the Lord*, 507.

Chapter 34

1. As cited in Bert Gary, *Jesus Unplugged: Provocative, Raw and Fully Exposed* (Grand Haven, Mich.: FaithWalk Publishing, 2005), 15-16.

2. Gail T. Fairhurst and Robert A. Sarr, *The Art of Framing: Managing the Language of Leadership* (San Francisco: Jossey-Bass, 1996), talk about the "skill" and "power" of framing.

3. George Lakoff, *Don't Think of an Elephant: Know Your Values and Frame the Debate* (White River Junction, Vt.: Chelsea Green, 2004), xv.

4. Culture Care Technologies, "Case Study 18: Making Change," http://culturecare.org.hosting.domaindirect.com/cases/case018.htm (accessed 16 February 2006).

5. Michel Serres, in *Rameaux* (Le Pommier, 2005), approaches "languages and myths as 'formatting' cultural and ethical life," sometimes on a religious grid, sometimes on a scientific grid, and sometimes on a "meshed amalgam." Quoted in Frederic Raphael, "*TLS* Books of the Year," *TLS: Times Literary Supplement*, 2 December 2005, 11. See also the French original: Michel Serres, *Rameaux* (Paris: Editions Le Pommier, 2004).

6. This is the thesis of David Brown, "The Role of Images in Theological Reflection," in *The Human Person in God's World: Studies to Commemorate the Austin Farrer Centenary*, ed. Brian Hebbelthwaite and Douglas Hedley (London: SCM Press, 2006), 85-205.

7. Nelson Goodman, *Ways of Worldmaking* (Indianapolis: Hackett Publishing, 1978).

8. See Rob Weber, *Imagesmiths* (Abingdon, 2006).

9. Quoted in Bharat Tandon, "The Smell of the Gulag," *TLS: Times Literary Supplement*, 29 September 2006, 22.

10. W. J. Thomas Mitchell, *What Do Pictures Want? The Lives and Loves of Images* (Chicago: University of Chicago Press, 2005), 10, 89-92.

11. Ibid., xv.

12. The Lakoff quotes are from George Lakoff, *Don't Think of an Elephant*, xv.

13. I got this idea from W. J. Thomas Mitchell, *What Do Pictures Want?* 9.